The
Modern
Wiccan's
GUIDE TO LIVING

The Modern Wiccan's GUIDE TO LIVING

WITH WITCHY RITUALS AND SPELLS FOR LOVE, LUCK, WELLNESS, AND PROSPERITY

Cerridwen Greenleaf

CICO BOOKS
LONDON NEW YORK

"Pick up your rattle, pack up your dreams.
We'll walk hand-in-hand in a magical land."

Luisah Teish

**This book is for all the grandmothers, wise women, elders, crones
and other women who have passed down the wisdom we use today.
Eternal love and gratitude.**

This edition published in 2020 by CICO Books
An imprint of Ryland Peters & Small Ltd

20–21 Jockey's Fields   341 E 116th St
London WC1R 4BW   New York, NY 10029
www.rylandpeters.com

First published in 2019

10 9 8 7 6 5 4 3 2

Text in this book has previously appeared in
5-Minute Magic for Modern Wiccans and *The Book
of Kitchen Witchery*.

A CIP catalog record for this book is available from the
Library of Congress and the British Library.

ISBN: 978-1-78249-883-4

Printed in China

Editors: Sophie Elletson and Jennifer Jahn
Photographer and stylist: Belle Daughtry
Illustrator: Emma Garner

Commissioning editor: Kristine Pidkameny
Senior editor: Carmel Edmonds
Designers: Emily Breen and Eliana Holder
Art director: Sally Powell
Production: David Hearn
Publishing manager: Penny Craig
Publisher: Cindy Richards

Safety note: Please note that while the use of
essential oils, herbs, incense, and particular
practices refer to healing benefits, they are not
intended to replace diagnosis of illness or ailments,
or healing or medicine. Always consult your doctor
or other health professional in the case of illness,
pregnancy, and personal sensitivities and
conditions. Neither the author nor the publisher
can be held responsible for any claim arising out of
the general information, recipes, and practices
provided in the book.

CONTENTS

THE CHARMED LIFE

Every witch walks the spiritual path with practical feet, navigating the modern world aided by ancient wisdom. When you begin to access this special knowledge, you join a lineage of folks who are more in tune with the natural world around us—our Mother Earth, the moon and the stars, herbs and plants. In its essence, Wicca is a wisdom tradition intended to aid our evolution, both individually and communally. It helps us maintain spiritual harmony with the earth and beyond, while also balancing our relationships with others.

The spells and ritual work in this book cover the gamut of magical rites and charms that you can apply to every aspect of your life: health, wealth, work, creativity, home and family, self-care, and love. There's truly something for everyone, from beginners to those of you who are very advanced in your wielding of the craft.

As you seek a sacred life, know that everything you do can be a vessel to carry enchantment: each seed you plant, every tea you brew. There is great joy in this, along with great responsibility. Magic is about far more than the spoken words of spells. The greater the clarity of intention, the more powerful your conjuring will be. Before you begin using any of the spells contained herein, think about the words and your intention, gathering energy from a place deep within.

Magic resides inside us; we create it with our thoughts and actions. It is our deepest power and we are all born with it. It is how we make things better for ourselves, for our friends and loved ones, and for our community and our world. This book is designed with you in mind, to encourage and empower you to live life to the fullest and, most importantly, to access the wisdom that comes so naturally to you.

CHAPTER 1

TOOLS OF THE TRADE

All the Essentials

Your tools collect and hold the magic that lives inside you.
They will become instilled with your energy and become a source
of power for you and magnify the strength of your ritual work.
Plus, metaphysical must-haves are around every corner—amazing
candles and essential oils at the grocer, pharmacy, and apothecary
store, as well as incense, herbs, and crystals aplenty at the mind-body
bookshop and health-food store. Additional tools at your disposal
are less tangible than knives, cauldrons, herbs, and wands; these are
your breath, visualization, and intuition, which will help you focus
your thoughts and emotions. Your intention purifies all these
extra skills in your arsenal.

A Kitchen Witch's Toolkit

You'll find that you already own some of the kitchen witch's basic tools, but you may want to acquire new-to-you items whose sole use will be for kitchen magic.

✳

BROOM ETIQUETTE

This is very important—do not use your ritual broom for housecleaning. Like me, you may well view every inch of your home as sacred space, but you will need to keep your regular housekeeping implements separate from those you use for your magical workings. Think of it as a separation of church and state, if you will. It pretty much is!

In general, it is not advisable to use tools such as your ritual knife to debone a chicken, for example, as this risks a confusing blending of mundane and magical energies. If you treat your ritual tools with the utmost respect, they will serve you very well. Over time, they will become inculcated with magic through exclusive use in your ritual workings. The Wiccan tradition holds brooms in high regard, and some witches have an impressive collection of brooms, each one named to distinguish their roles as "familiars," or kindred spirits. Kitchen witches often have the most extensive bevy of brooms of anyone.

Broom

This magical tool was born centuries ago from the practical magic of sweeping the ritual area clean before casting a spell. With focus and intention, you can dispel negative influences and bad spirits from the area and prepare a space for ritual work. In bygone days, pagan marriages and Beltane trysts took place with a leap over the broom, an old-fashioned tradition of handfasting, the classic witch wedding. Over the centuries, this rich history began to capture the imagination as the archetypal symbol of witches.

Your broom is an essential tool for energy management. Obtain a handmade broom from a craft fair or your favorite metaphysical five-and-dime. This should not be a machine-made plastic one from the supermarket, although I did get a long cinnamon-infused rush broom from Trader Joe's that I use in my witch's kitchen. A broom made of wood and woven of natural straw will be imbued with the inherent energies of those organic materials.

Crafting Your Own Purification Broom

To purify your space with as much of your own personal energy as possible, a broom you have crafted by hand is best. You don't have to wait until you are holding a circle or performing spellcraft—you can purify after a squabble with a loved one, or to rid yourself of a bout of the blues, or any upset you need to sweep right out of your home. Many a kitchen witch begins the day with this simple ritual of a clean sweep to freshen surroundings and to make room for good energy in your life. Of course, this cleaning is not intended to make your house spotless; it is a symbolic act that is effective in maintaining your home as a personal sanctuary.

You can make your own purification broom from straw bound together and attached to a fallen tree branch, or you can add some mojo to a store-bought broom. Wrap copper wire around the bottom of your broom handle and also use it to bind straw to a sturdy stick or branch for the DIY kind. Venus-ruled copper lends an aura of beauty and keeps negativity at bay. Attach crystals to the handle with glue to boost your broom's power (see below).

Crystals for Your Broom

* **Amber** for good cheer
* **Blue lace agate** for tranquility and a peaceful home
* **Coral** for well-being
* **Jet** absorbs bad energy
* **Onyx** is a stone of protection
* **Petrified wood** for security
* **Tiger's eye** will protect you from energy-draining situations or people
* **Turquoise** creates calm and relaxation

Cauldron

Here we have a true essential for kitchen witchery! The cauldron represents the goddess; its round basin is symbolic of the womb from which we all came. Ideally made of cast iron or another durable metal that heats uniformly, the cauldron can hold fire and represents rebirth, the phoenix rising from the ashes of the past. Usually, cauldrons stand on three legs for practicality, stability, and mobility. You can place one on your kitchen altar if there is room or on the floor to the left of the altar.

In spring, this sacred basin can be used to hold earth or water and, in the winter season, it should hold fire—candle flames or sweet-smoked incense, which signifies the rebirth of the sun to come at the end of the coldest season. You can also be playful with the form the cauldron takes and use a rain-filled urn or a flower-filled fountain. Summer's cauldron can be a beautiful cup; at harvest-time, use a pumpkin or another hollowed-out gourd. You can play with the vessel concept in your own ceremonies and be imaginative—get really creative.

A classic cast-iron cauldron is very useful for mixing your herbs and essential oils—just make sure to clean it thoroughly after each use so as not to mix energies inadvertently. You can scry with a cauldron full of water to foresee the future by reading images on the surface of the water, as well as use this magical vessel for burning papers upon which you have written spells, incantations, and magical intentions. In doing this, you are sending your wishes to the gods and goddesses through the flames, the element of Fire.

Chalice

The chalice—another vessel symbolizing the feminine, the Goddess and fertility—is a goblet dedicated specially for use on your altar. Holding both physical fluid and waters of our emotional body, it is connected to the element of Water. Place your carefully chosen chalice on the left side of your altar with all other representations of the energy of the female and the Goddess. A grail is also a chalice. Legend tells that the Holy Grail brought life back to the decaying kingdom of Camelot and restored King Arthur and his people to health, giving rise to the rebirth of England itself. On your altar, your chalice can hold water, mead, wine, juice, or anything that has been blessed. It can contain holy water for consecrations and blessing rites. At the end of many ritual ceremonies and sabbats, it is customary to toast the deities with a hearty ale, cider, or wine and thank them for being present. After the circle has been opened, you can pour the contents of your chalice into the ground outdoors as an offering to benevolent entities.

Magic Bottles

Spell bottles, or magic bottles, have been around since the 1600s and were often filled with hair, nails, blood, and other kind of ephemera. Now, they are used to empower us and adorn our sacred spaces. Though their popularity has waned since the Elizabethan age when they were called "witch bottles," they are still used for a variety of intentions, and your magical kitchen can display many a spell bottle. You can customize your own spell-in-a-bottle with crystal stoppers and you should let your imagination run wild as to the usage and positive purposes with which you can fill your vessels: put one in your garden to keep your plants healthy, one in the bedroom to bring love and happiness, and a spell bottle on the living room mantel to protect your home. Spell bottles are used for protection primarily, but you can also put symbols of your dreams and desires in them—cinnamon for the spice of life, a rose for romance, rosemary for remembrance.

Pendulum

A pendulum is a witchy tool that helps with decision making. Pendulums are easily bought at any metaphysical or New Age shop or mind, body, spirit bookstore, but you can also make your own, with a 12-inch (30cm) strip of string or leather cord and a small rose quartz with a pointy end. Knot the quartz onto your cord and test it to show you which is "Yes" and which is "No." This is done by asking it yes/no questions that you know the answer to, then observing its responses—you will notice it swings in a different way for each one, for example, round in a circle clockwise or counterclockwise, or back and forth.

SPELL BOTTLE SECRETS

To ensure that your kitchen is peaceful, secure, and grounded in "good vibrations," gather a teaspoon of clean, dry soil from outside your home and put it into a bottle with smoky quartz crystal, brown jasper, or any dark, earthen-colored semiprecious stone. Place the bottle in a potted herb on your windowsill and think about the sanctity of your space every time you water your plant. As your plant grows and thrives, so will the tranquility of your space.

A bottle with a rosebud or rose petal, rose essential oil, and rose quartz next to your bedside will help with love. For six days, rub oil from the bottle onto a pink candle and burn it for one hour. On the seventh day, your romantic prospects will brighten.

For luck with money, place three pennies and some pyrite, green jade, or peridot in a bottle and put it on your desk or workspace. At least three times a day, visualize a lot of money and shake the magic money bottle. After three days, your fortunes will improve.

Bowls

While a bowl is not a tool in and of itself, you can utilize bowls in your spell work often and anytime you are inspired to do so. Clear, glass bowls are regularly used.

Blessing Bowl Ritual

*These waters cleanse my
soul and being,
Now, with a clear mind and
heart, I am seeing,
I am love; my heart is as big
as sky and earth.
From the east to the west,
love universal gives life its worth.
Blessings to all, so mote it be.*

Three simple ingredients—a red rose, a pink candle, and water—can bestow a powerful blessing. The rose signifies beauty, potential, the sunny seasons, love for yourself and others. The candle stands for the element of Fire, the yellow flame of the rising sun in the east, harmony, higher intention, and the light of the soul. Water represents its own element, flow, the direction of the west, emotions, and cleansing. This ritual can be performed alone or with a group in which you pass the bowl around.

Float the rose in a clear bowl of water and light a pink candle beside the bowl. With your left hand, gently stir the water in the bowl and say the words on the left.

Athame

Pronounced "a-tha-may," this is your magical knife. It can also be a ritual dagger or sword. The athame represents and contains yang energy, the male aspect of the deities. Ritual knifes are also associated with the element of Fire. For these two reasons, your ritual knife should be placed on the right side of your altar. It is to be used to direct the energies raised in your circles and spellwork; because it is not used for cutting but rather for the manipulation of the forces involved in the work of enchantment, an athame is usually a dull blade. The knives you use to slice bread and chop veggies are in a completely different category. Some Wiccan traditionalists specify that the handle of the athame should be black or very dark in color (as in the artwork above opposite), since black is the color that absorbs energies and, therefore, becomes quickly attuned to the practitioner.

Bolline

A bolline, pronounced "bowl-in," is most often a white-handled knife (as in the artwork to the right) that is used for making other tools and for cutting materials such as cords and herbs within the sacred circle. You can create your own magic wand, for example, by cutting a tree branch with your bolline. This increases the energy held within the wand and creates a magical tool by using a magical tool. You can also use your bolline for carving symbols and names into your candles and wands as well as your other tools. A bolline generally has a curved blade and a white handle to distinguish it from the athame, and it is also associated with male energy.

Wand

A magical wand is a powerful tool used to cast a magic circle (see page 23) and invoke deities. Like an athame, a wand focuses projects and directs energy. Because it gathers and stores magical power, a wand is wonderful for healing and can be the device with which you draw the shape when you cast the circle.

If possible, find your wand in a serendipitous manner. Draw it to yourself through attraction. A wand makes a mighty gift. If it feels really right to you, you can and should purchase your own wand. Just be sure to purify it, cleansing the energy of the shop so it is truly yours. However, before you take off for the next metaphysical five-and-dime, take a walk in the woods closest to where you reside. You may very well find the wand of your dreams waiting for you on the forest floor. Find out more about making your own wand on page 22. The most important factor for any wand is how it "feels" in your hand. You will know immediately when you have found the right one.

Candles

The popularity of candles has reached an all-time high. Candles are used by folks from all walks of life for relaxation, meditation, aromatherapy, and, most importantly, to achieve that "peaceful homey" feeling of being in your own sanctuary. This simple yet profound tool can make powerful magic. Take a moment and notice how candlelight transforms a dark room and fills the atmosphere with the energy of magical light. Suddenly the potential for transformation is evident. Every candle contains all four elements:

* Air—Oxygen feeds and fans the candle flame
* Earth—Solid wax forms the body of the candle
* Water—Melting wax represents the fluid elemental state
* Fire—The flame sparks and blazes

How to Charge a Candle

Charging a candle means instilling it with magical intent. A candle that has been charged fills your personal space with intention and expands it into all four elements and into the celestial sphere. Ritual candles are chosen for their color correspondences and are carved, "dressed," or anointed with special oils chosen for their particular energy.

Once you clarify your intention, cleanse your candles by passing them through the purifying smoke of sage or incense. Further charge your candle by carving a symbol into the wax. You can warm the tip of your ritual knife using a lit match and carve your full intention into the candle wax. As you engrave the appropriate magical works onto the candle, you are charging it with energy and the hope and purpose of your spell. Some highly successful examples of this that I have used and witnessed in circle gatherings are:

* "Healing for my friend who is in the hospital; she will recover with renewed and increased health."
* "I get the raise I am asking for, and more!"
* "New true love enters my life in the coming season, blessed be."

A QUICK GUIDE TO CANDLE-COLOR MAGIC

Green: money, prosperity, growth, luck, jobs, gardening, youth, beauty, fertility

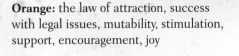

Orange: the law of attraction, success with legal issues, mutability, stimulation, support, encouragement, joy

Dark blue: change, flexibility, the unconscious, psychic powers, emotional healing

Light blue: patience, happiness, triumph over depression, calm, deep understanding, compassion

Pink: love, friendship, kindness, faithfulness, goodness, affection

Red: strength, protection, sexuality, vitality, passion, courage, heart, intense feelings of love, good health, power

Brown: home, animal wisdom, grounding, physical healing

White: purification, peace, protection from negativity, truth, binding, sincerity, serenity, chastity, gladness, spirit

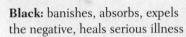

Black: banishes, absorbs, expels the negative, heals serious illness

Purple: female power, stress relief, ambition, healing past wounds, goddess-hood, business success

Gold: solar magic, money, attraction, the astral plane

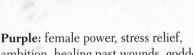

Gray: neutrality, impasses, cancellation

Yellow: mental power and vision, intelligence, clear thinking, study, self-assurance, prosperity, divination, psychism, abundance, wisdom, power of persuasion, charisma, sound sleep

Next, you should "dress" your candle with a specific oil. Every essential oil is imbued with a power that comes from the plants and flowers of which it is made. You can also use oils to anoint yourself at the crown of the head or at the third eye to increase mental clarity. By using the inherent powers of essential oils and anointing both your tool and yourself, you are increasing and doubling the energies, in this case the candle and yourself.

Essential oils are highly concentrated extracts of flowers, herbs, roots, or resin extract, sometimes diluted in neutral-base oil. Try to ensure you are using natural oils instead of manufactured, chemical-filled perfume oil; the synthetics lack any real energy. Also, approach oils with caution and don't get them in your eyes. Clean cotton gloves are a good idea to keep in your witch's kitchen for handling sensitive materials. You can avoid any mess and protect your magical tools by using oil droppers. Do not use essential oils in the first trimester of pregnancy and consult an aromatherapist if using in the later stages. Find a trusted herbalist or the wise sage at your local metaphysical shop; usually they can offer much in the way of helpful knowledge.

Magical Meanings of Essential Oils

* **Healing:** bay, cedar wood, cilantro (coriander), cinnamon, eucalyptus, juniper, lime, rose, sandalwood, spearmint

* **Prosperity:** aloe, basil, cinnamon, clove, ginger, nutmeg, oakmoss, orange, patchouli, peppermint, pine

* **Love:** apricot, basil, chamomile, cilantro (coriander), clove, copal, geranium, jasmine, lemon, lime, neroli, rose, rosemary, ylang-ylang

* **Sexuality:** amber, cardamom, clove, lemongrass, olive, patchouli, rose

* **Peace:** chamomile, lavender

* **Luck:** nutmeg, orange, rose, vervain

* **Courage:** black pepper, frankincense, geranium

* **Joy:** bergamot, lavender, neroli, vanilla

* **Divination:** camphor, clove, orange

* **Astral projection:** benzoin, cinnamon, jasmine, sandalwood

* **Dispelling negative energy and spirits:** basil, clove, copal, frankincense, juniper, myrrh, peppermint, pine, rosemary, Solomon's seal, vervain, yarrow

* **Protection:** anise, bay, black pepper, cedar wood, clove, copal, cypress, eucalyptus, frankincense, juniper, lavender, lime, myrrh, rose geranium, sandalwood, vetiver

* **Enchantment:** amber, apple, ginger, tangerine

Censer

A censer, pronounced "sen-ser" and also known as a thurible, is an incense burner and represents the elements of Air and Fire. Place your incense at the very center of your altar. Incense offers a way to bless your space and also to purify with the sacred smoke—your tools, your ritual circle, your mind. The evocative scent and soft, billowing smoke will transport you in a sensory way. Nowadays, there is an incredible variety of incense burners available, so follow your instincts as to what is best for your kitchen altar— perhaps a smoking dragon or a goddess holding the fiery embers of your incense would add greatly to the energy of your altar.

It is a good idea to test your incense before using it in ritual, especially before organizing a group circle, to see how much smoke is produced to avoid any problems; and it's best to check with your fellow participants to make sure no one has any special sensitivities. One of my dearest and nearest gets migraines whenever any amber is used— candles, oils, incense. If you find you can't burn incense for any such reason, you can use another Air symbol instead, such as feathers, potpourri, fresh flowers, or even a paper fan.

Incense itself contains inherent energies that you can use to augment your intention and further power your magical purpose. I have learned much about different kinds of incense—loose, cone, stock, and cylinder— as well as the best kinds of herbs to use through experimentation, asking elders, and observing magi at work. Overleaf are two of my favorite incense recipes.

Circle Incense

4 parts frankincense

2 parts myrrh

2 parts benzoin

1 part sandalwood

1 part cinnamon

1 part rose petals

1 part vervain

1 part rosemary

1 part bay leaf

1 part orange peel

This incense will significantly aid the formation of the sphere of energy
that is the ritual circle (see page 23). Each part is a heaping teaspoon
in my recipes but you can change that if you are making larger
batches. A fine grind of all the ingredients is the key to good incense,
so you should add a pestle and mortar to your kitchen
if you plan to make a lot of incense.

Clearing Incense

3 parts myrrh

3 parts copal

3 parts frankincense

1 part sandalwood

This is an optimal mixture of essences to purify your home or sacred
working space. Negative energies are vanquished and the path is
cleared for ritual. Open windows and doors when you are burning this
cleaning incense so the bad can be released outside and dissipate. It is
advisable to use this recipe if there are arguments or any other kind of
disruptions in your home. You can create sanctuary with this incense.

Book of Shadows

Here we have your kitchen witch's recipe record, a ledger for all your magical workings, including spells, rituals, and results. This is your journal of all you have practiced and wrought as well as your research. Are your spells more effective during the new moon in the water signs of Cancer, Pisces, or Scorpio? That may well be unique to you and as you arrive at these important discoveries, you should write them down in your Book of Shadows so you know your true power as tested by time. This is not just a ledger though, it is a living document that you can apply to magical workings to come and will even help you design your own spells and ritual recipes. All the astrology, herb lore, crystal properties, lunar signs, and seasonal information will come into play as you experiment and uncover what works best for you. By keeping my own Book of Shadows, I was able to conclude that, for me, the new moon in Pisces is a super-powered time for my spells.

This is a book you will turn to again and again and your Book of Shadows should be very appealing to you. It can be a gorgeous, one-of-a-kind volume made with handmade paper and uniquely tooled bindings, or it can be a simple three-ring binder. Choose whatever is most useful to you.

"The human heart longs for ritual—to be fully alive and whole. We must engage in rites of passage."

Make Your Own Manifestation Tool

A wand is used for directing energy. It is best to make your own wand from found wood and instill it with your personal energy. You could go out into a nearby park or the woods and find a suitable branch that has fallen. Never cut a wand straight from a tree as the energy from harm to the tree will be retained by the wand. Allow Mother Nature to choose one for you; she is always right. You might find the perfect weathered wand on a beach as driftwood.

A found piece of wood (see suggestions below)

Sand paper

Bolline

12 inches (30cm) copper wire

A crystal of your preference to use as the pointer (see page 166 for suggestions)

Beads, sequins, seashells, tiny crystals, or other decorations of your choice

When you have found the perfect piece of wood, sand it to smoothness so it feels good in your hand, which is very important. If your found wood branch is too long, use your magical bolline knife to cut it down to 12 inches (30cm), or your preferred length. Wrap copper wire around the top and affix your crystal to the end. Your wand should look beautiful to your eye so embellish it with ornaments you love, such as beads, sequins, seashells, tiny crystals, or whatever pleases you and adds to the power of this sacred implement.

When choosing wood for your wand, remember that each tree has distinctive properties:

* **Birch** (*Betula pendula*) has feminine energy and healing power. Boiled soft birch wood was traditionally used to soothe bruises and calm cuts. Use a birch wand for healing spells, for calming situations, and for requesting a diplomatic solution.

* **Crab apple** (*Malus sylvestris*) will provide bent, gnarled wands. The apple tree, as we know, is the tree of knowledge and wisdom. Apples, the fruit and the wood, are extremely useful to witchcraft. Use an apple wand whenever you need guidance, want to know the truth, or simply as an everyday wand.

* **Rowan** or **mountain ash** (*Sorbus aucuparia*) is native to the British Isles. There is a closely related American species, *Sorbus Americana*. It's a "portal tree," and therefore when you want to undertake a journey or a guided visualization, keep your mountain-ash wand close by.

* **Oak** (*Quercus robur*) has a strong masculine energy and is good for healing and protection. It makes a long-lasting wand for intensely focused work. If you choose to use only one wand, make it oak.

There are other suggestions for materials to make wands in this book—see pages 86 and 150.

Bringing Magic into Your Life

When you establish a sacred space, such as your altar, and use your magical tools in it, you can create a place where the mundane world is left behind. It can be in your home or your backyard where, despite the noise of the day-to-day, you can touch the sacred. Anywhere you choose can become a circle of magic and you can create one anywhere by "casting," or drawing in the air with concentrated energy with a wand or athame. Inside this circle, energy is raised, rituals are performed, and spells are worked. The sacred space is also where you call upon the gods and goddesses and become attuned to your own special desires. With attention and focus, working in the circle can be a truly marvelous experience. All your senses will come alive. You will feel, see, and hear the energies that you invoke. You will have created a tangible sphere of power.

Trust your intuition, go with your instincts,
and listen to your heart.

By following these three simple guidelines, you will craft beautiful, and more importantly, meaningful rituals to enrich your life, provide comfort, and maintain harmony and balance in your life. Personal ritual benefits you the most when it adapts to your current needs. Whether you need serenity, prosperity, more love in your life or swift change, the spells in this book will help you get there.

CHAPTER 2

MAGIC IN THE HOME

Creating a Sanctuary Space

Your home should feel like a retreat from the world. You should be able to walk in the front door and immediately feel comfortable. In focusing your attention on your living space, you'll discover what might be holding you back from being utterly happy there, and be able to use this wisdom to conjure pure contentment. Creating a personal altar offers a place to incubate your ideas, hopes, and intentions. It can become a touchstone for morning blessings and simple daily rituals that will maximize good energy around you. Your garden, whether it is a balcony full of blooms or a plot out back, can also offer a haven, a place where your spirit is renewed and restored. Growing herbs and plants to use in remedies and spellcraft is doubly rewarding; with each passing season, you will grow in your wisdom and skill.

Your Personal Power Center

Before there were temples and churches, the primary place for expressing reverence was the altar. The word "altar" comes from the Latin, meaning "high." With a personal altar, you can reach the heights of your spiritual ascension in wisdom.

You construct an altar when you assemble symbolic items in a meaningful manner and focus both your attention and your intention. When you work with the combined energies of these items, you are performing a ritual. Your rituals can arise from your needs, imagination, or the seasonal and traditional ceremonies that you find in this book and others. A book from which I draw much inspiration has been Nancy Brady Cunningham's *A Book of Women's Altars*, and I love her advice to bow or place your hands on the ground in front of your altar at the beginning of ritual work and at the closing. She explains that "Grounding symbolizes the end of the ritual and signals to the mind to return to an ordinary state of awareness as you re-enter daily life." An altar is a physical point of focus for the ritual, containing items considered sacred and essential to ritual work and spiritual growth. An altar can be anything from a rock in the forest to an exquisitely carved antique table. Even portable or temporary altars can suffice, such as a board suspended between two chairs for "rituals on the go."

Creating a Kitchen Altar

On a low table or chest of your choosing, place a forest-green cloth and a brown candle to represent family and home. Add lovely objects you have gathered, including items from the garden and the outdoors: ocean-carved driftwood, a gorgeous flower, a dried seedpod, a favorite crystal—whatever pleases your eye. It is of the utmost importance to add a bouquet of wildflowers native to your area, which you should have gathered close to where you live or bought locally. These posies will help integrate you and your home into your neighborhood and geographic region. Add a sweetly scented sachet of herbs from your kitchen garden or those you intend to plant—for example, rosemary, lavender, thyme, or mint, all of which imbue your space with positive energy. Find more suggestions on page 28. Burn associated essential oils, choosing those which will create an aura of comfort around your kitchen, including vanilla, cinnamon, or sweet-orange neroli in an oil lamp.

Finally, anoint the brown candle, concentrating on the power of peace and bliss surrounding your home and all around your kitchen altar. Chant the words below:

Peace and plenty are in abundance
And here true bliss surrounds,
From now on, all disharmony is gone,
This is a place of powerful blessings
For here lives sheer joy.
And so it is—blessed be!

This consecrated space will ease your spirits at any time. Your altar connects you to the earth of which you are a part.

Sanctuary Spell

To anoint your home and turn it into a protective shield for you and your loved ones, rub any of the following essential oils on your doorjambs— cinnamon, clove, dragon's blood, myrrh. Walk through the door into your home and close it securely. Take the remaining essential oils and rub a little on all other doors and windows. Light anointed white candles and place them in the windows and chant the words of the spell on the right.

My home is my temple.
Here I live and love,
Safe and secure,
Both below and above.
And so it is by magic sealed.

Kitchen Magic Altar Herbs

* **Cinnamon** refreshes and directs spirituality; it is a protection herb and handy for healing, money, love, sensuality, personal power, and success with work and creative projects.

* **Clove** is good for bringing money to you and for helping evade negative energies and block them.

* **Lavender** is a potent healer that calms and aids deep rest and dreams.

* **Myrrh** has been considered to be very sacred since ancient times and will intensify your spirituality. It also wards off bad spirits.

* **Nutmeg** is a lucky herb that promotes good health and abundance. It also encourages loyalty and marital fidelity.

* **Peppermint** is an herb of purification and increases psychic powers. Mint brings relaxation and can help you sleep, reducing anxiety.

* **Rosemary** purifies and increases memory and intelligence. This savory plant also heightens sensuality and bonds of love. It will also keep you youthful!

* **Sage** brings wisdom, health, and a long life. It is very useful for dispelling negative vibrations and encouraging cleansing. Sage can help your wishes come true, too.

* **Star anise** aids divination and psychic abilities.

* **Tonka bean** will give you courage and draws love and money.

* **Vanilla** is an herb of love and expands and enriches your mental capacity.

Pot of Gold: Abundance Altar Blessing

Cauldron magic is more about the acts of brewing something new than it is about purification by water. To attract money, fill a big pot with fresh water and place it on your altar during the waxing moon. Pour a cup of milk with a tablespoon of honey and a tablespoon of ground cloves into the pot as an offering. Toss handfuls of dried chamomile, moss, and vervain into the vessel. With your head raised high, say aloud:

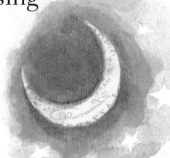

I call upon you, gods and goddesses of old, to fill my purse with gold.
I offer you mother's milk and honey sweet.
With harm to none and blessings to thee, I honor you for bringing
me health and prosperity.

Place the offering bowl on your altar and leave the aromatic mixture there to instill your kitchen with the energy of abundance. After four hours and forty-four minutes, go outside your home and pour the offering into your kitchen garden or into the roots of a shrub. Then bow in appreciation of the kindness of the gods and goddesses.

✳

FLORAL FUNDING

The following list of plants can be used in any ritual work whose intention is prosperity: allspice, almond, basil, bergamot, cedar leaves, cinnamon, cinquefoil, clover, dill, ginger, heliotrope, honeysuckle, hyssop, jasmine, mint, myrtle, nutmeg, oak moss, sassafras, vervain, and woodruff. Try these alone or in mixtures, tinctures, or grind into your incenses. You can also plant a prosperity garden and refresh your abundance altar with herbs and flowers grown by your own hand.

Gratitude Prayer Spell

Gratitude is not only uplifting but feels wonderful. There is powerful magic in recognizing all that you possess.

Timing: When moon or sun is in the sign of Taurus it is the time of prosperity and security. Time this ritual for a Thursday during that lunar or solar sign as Thursday is "Thor's Day" and the day of abundance. It is also the perfect time to acknowledge the gifts of life.

Sit in a comfortable position and close your eyes. Think about your blessings. What are you grateful for at this moment? Breathe steadily and deeply, inhaling and exhaling slowly for a few minutes. Now pray aloud:

Good gods and Goddess, giver of all the fruits of this earth,
Thank you for all bounty, beauty, and well-being,
Bless all who give and receive these gifts.
I am made of sacred earth, purest water, sacred fire,
and wildest wind.
Blessings upon me. Blessings upon we and thee.
So mote it be.

Record your blessings in a journal or in your Book of Shadows. You should perform this gratitude prayer spell periodically and look back at your blessings and reflect upon them. This is also a wonderful grace to say at the family meal to offer thanks for all we are given.

Floral Fortification: Vesta's Hearth Offering

The sign of Cancer is very much oriented toward love of home and family as well as security. Mixed dried flowers, otherwise known as potpourri, are now a popular household staple. It was a medieval custom to have them in the house, revived by the Victorians. Use different combinations for desired magical results; they help create sacred sanctuary space.

1 cup (20g) of dried rose petals

1 cup (20g) of dried marigold

1 cup (20g) of dried lily petals

A basket or bowl for the flower blend

Clove essential oil

Cinnamon essential oil

Timing: Either sun or moon in Cancer is a perfect time for this offering to the goddess of happy homes.

Put all the dried posies in the basket or bowl and sprinkle them with the essential oils. Place the mixture on the south point of your altar for the duration of a moon cycle. The sweet and spicy scent of the potpourri will spread a positive and protective energy to your home and your magical workings. A wreath of these same flowers with garlic cloves added will protect you from harm and illness. If you are a working witch, a small, sweet-smelling bowl of potpourri on your desk will provide constant comfort. If you have a fireplace, keep some on the mantle as an offering to the domestic goddess Vesta, she who keeps the home fire burning. When the scent has faded, burn it in your cast iron cauldron or a fireplace as an offering to her. Speak this invocation when making the offering:

Vesta, goddess of home and hearth,
Stand guard over this place I love.
Keep safe the ones I love.
This night, we breathe in peace.
These flowers are my offering to you.
So mote it be.

Power Potpourri

¼ cup (5g) dried rosemary

4 dried bay laurel leaves

⅛ cup (5g) dried sage

1 teaspoon dried juniper berries

Simmer this mixture in a pot of water on your stove whenever you feel the need to infuse your space with protection or want an energetic turnaround from negative to positive. A bad day at work, family squabble, an unfortunate incident in your neighborhood: instead of just muddling along, you can do something about it, and your creation of the positive will help you and your loved ones as well as your neighbors. This power potpourri will also safeguard you from outside influences that can be disruptive. Set your intention before gathering the herbs from your stores.

Mix the herbs together by hand. While you are sifting them through your fingers, close your eyes and visualize your home protected by a boundary of glowing white light. Imagine the light running through you to the herbs in your hand and charging them with the energy of safety, sanctity, and protection. Add the herbs to slowly simmering water and breathe in the newly charged air.

Stone Altar Spell: Burning Away Bad Luck

Your home is your safe space. Yet the world is constantly coming in and bringing mundane energy over your threshold—problems at the workplace, financial woes, bad news from your neighborhood or the world at large. All this negativity wants to get in the way and stay. While you can't do anything about the stock market crash in China or a co-worker's divorce, you can do something about not allowing this bad energy to cling to you by using this home-keeping spell. The best times to release any and all bad luck are on a Friday 13th or on any waxing moon. As you know, Friday 13th is considered a lucky day on the witch's calendar.

Get a big black candle and a black crystal, a piece of white paper, a black pen with black ink, and a cancellation stamp, readily available at any stationery store. Go into your backyard or a nearby park or woodlands and find a flat rock that has a slightly concave surface. Using the pen, write down on the white paper that of which you want to rid yourself and your home; this is your release request. Place the candle and the black crystal on the rock; light the candle, and while it burns, intone the words of the spell on the right.

Visualize a clear and peaceful home filled with only positivity as the candle burns for 13 minutes. Stamp the paper with the cancel stamp. Snuff the candle, fold the paper away from your body, and place it under the rock. Speak your thanks to the moon for assisting you. If you have a truly serious issue at hand, repeat the process for 13 nights and all will be vanquished.

Waxing moon, most wise Selene,
From me this burden please dispel
Upon this night so clear and bright
I release ___ to the moon tonight.

"The more use an altar gets, the more energy it builds up, making your spells even more effective and powerful."

Salt of the Earth Blessing Spell

Every house has a box of salt. This most common of seasonings is essential to physical health and also to the health of your home. With a bowl of salt alone, you can purify your home every day and have a "safe zone" for ritual work. You can leave a bowl of pure salt in any room you feel is in need of freshening; the salt absorbs negativity. Many a witch uses this homely approach on a daily basis early in the day, tidying up and cleansing energy to charge the home with positivity.

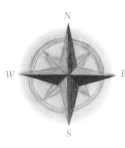

In your kitchen, take a bowl of water, freshly drawn, and a small cup of salt. Take the vessel of water and sprinkle in as much salt as you feel is needed. Anoint your fingers by dipping them in the salt water and then touch your forehead around your third eye in the middle of your forehead.

Now turn to the east and say:

Power of the East,
Source of the Sun rising,
Bring me new beginnings.

After speaking, sprinkle some of the water in the eastern part of your kitchen.

Face south and say:

Source of the Starry Cross,
Place of warmth and light,
Bring me joy and bounty.

Scatter droplets of salt water in the southern direction.

Face the west and speak aloud:

Powers of the West,
Source of oceans, mountains,
and deserts all,
Bring me the security of the ground
beneath my feet.

Scatter droplets of water in the west side of your kitchen.

Face north now and speak aloud:

Powers of the North,
Bringer of winds and the polestar,
Show me vision and insight.

Sprinkle water in the northern area of the room.

End this ritual by sprinkling water and salt all around your home, especially around windows, sills, doorways, and thresholds where energy passes in and out as visitors and delivery people come and go. In this way, you are cleansing and managing the energy of your space. After a distressing occurrence, you can repeat this ritual and then leave a bowl of salt out for 24 hours so it can rid your sacred space of negative "vibes."

Kitchen Warming Spell

When you or a friend move into a new home, place a wreath on the front door and also on the outside of the kitchen or back door (if your kitchen doesn't lead directly outside). Gather two bundles of dried hops or eucalyptus, tie them with green and brown ribbons, and hang them high on the door. Walk through each door with a brown candle in a glass votive jar and aromatic cinnamon incense. Intone these words:

House of my body, I accept your shelter.
Home of my heart, I receive your blessings.
Home of my heart, I am open to joy.
And so it is. And so it shall be.

Incense Alchemy

Long ago, shamans and witches discovered that perfumed resins from herbs and tree branches could be thrown into the fire to release their properties. Ever since then, incense has been an essential tool in magical rites, recognized for its ability to restore universal equilibrium.

Making incense requires a mortar and pestle and a collection of 4-ounce (115ml) lidded jars. The incense is burned on small charcoal cakes, available at all metaphysical stores. Safe burning requires either a censer or use of a fireproof glass or clay dish.

Simple Incense Recipes

* **For peace of mind:** Crush sandalwood, bay leaves, and amber resin together. Burn a small amount on a charcoal cake in your fireproof glass or clay dish on your altar and meditate. The plant damania can be added to increase concentration.

* **For mastery of mind:** Crush together equal parts cinnamon and resinous benzoin. You will achieve your goals by burning this combination.

* **To enhance meditation:** Mix equal parts white sandalwood and frankincense, and add one-fourth part white orrisroot. Add a drop of oil from one of the following plants: angelica, agrimony, or aloe. Use this during the day of a full moon or during any lunar ceremony.

Herbal Helpers for Quick Protection Magic

You need look no further than your kitchen cabinet for other commonplace herbs to ward off unsettling energy:

* **Lemon rind:** When rubbed on furniture, doorjambs, and window frames, this cleanses negative energy.

* **Rosemary:** When added to potpourri, woven into a wreath, or sprinkled on your doorstep, this helps protect you.

* **Salt:** When sprinkled on the threshold of your home, this will keep away unwanted guests. (See also page 34.)

* **Kava kava:** Kava kava root guards against negative energy. Boil ground kava kava in a quart (1 liter) of water, let it cool and pour the water on your front step and walkway. To ramp the power up even more, add in 1 tablespoon each of ground cloves and cinnamon. Safety first!

Herbal Hex Breaker Ritual

Nothing can erode your inner calm more than being hexed or experiencing a run of bad luck and ill spirits. This foolproof spell requires you to obtain the bark of the wahoo plant from your herbalist. Known as *Euonymus atropurpureus*, it should never be ingested for any reason. Steep the bark in boiling water for 5 minutes. After it has cooled, dip your right index finger into the liquid and cross your forehead, saying seven times loudly, "Wahoo!" Whatever has been pestering you will leave your space immediately.

Cast Out All Ills: Floor Cleanser

Commercial cleansers are chock full of chemicals and potential toxins so I urge you to rethink using them. Simple herbal DIY cleaners are much healthier for you and your loved ones and always smell more natural. Who doesn't love the smell of lavender, citrus, and fresh mint?

A ceramic bowl

Hot water

1 quart (1 liter) of white vinegar

2 limes

2 lemons

A handful of fresh mint

6 drops lavender essential oil

A bucket

A clean mop

In a ceramic bowl, pour 2 cups (480ml) of hot water and half a cup (120ml) of lime and lemon juice, then add the fresh mint leaves and the lavender oil. Stir and let steep for a half hour, then strain out the leaves and compost them.

Take a clean bucket and fill it with two gallons of warm water, then pour in the essential oil mixture. Dip your mop into the bucket, wring it out, and clean the floor very thoroughly. Chant this charm as you use the mop:

Nothing but health and happiness here
Brightness and joy only remain in this sphere.
Anything dark and ill, I cast you out!
Harm to none, blessing throughout.

Awakened Breath Incantation

Unless you are already a practitioner of magical arts, you may well be casting spells unconsciously that throw obstacles in your path. Negative thoughts can imprint and start to manifest in an unfortunate way.

To clear the way to greater wealth and happiness, go for a walk during the next new moon. Pick up a white stone or white flower and place it on your altar. Light a white candle, and then close your eyes. Empty your mind and breathe deeply. Check to make sure your mind is not wandering; if any negative thoughts are lingering, send them out of your mind permanently.

After ten deep inhales and exhales, you should begin to feel a buzzing at the crown of your head. Now, open your eyes stare into the flame of the candle and repeat seven times:

I am alive.
I have power
It is real
And so it is.

Any time you find yourself engaged in negative self-talk or thinking, repeat this spell.

Supernatural Seeds and Herbs of Happiness

I have lived in homes where my only gardening options were containers on a deck or planters on the front stoop. This taught me that you can do a lot with seed packets, pots, and an open mind.

When selecting space for your garden you can have something as simple as a set of containers; this can be planned as with any other garden space. If you are lucky to have a backyard or land, I suggest you begin the designing process by incorporating all the plants you know and want to use in your magical workings and your cookery, and always allow yourself to experiment. Trying veggies or seeds that are new to you can be enormously rewarding. I agree with Londoner Alys Fowler, who is one of Britain's top gardeners. She says there is no earthly reason why roses and cabbages can't go side by side, and veggies can nicely nestle in among flowers. Once you have tried a few such painterly plantings, you can give yourself a free hand in your creative approach.

A witch's garden should have an aspect of wildness to it. Let the alyssum reseed itself and spread all over, creating a carpet of beauty. Allow the morning glory, jasmine, and nasturtiums to climb the fence with abandon. I encourage you to experiment and grow anything your heart desires. As the seasons pass, your garden will reflect your self-growth and will also be a haven you turn to for reflection.

Your Magical Intent

Do you use chamomile regularly? Do you purify your space with sage? Are rosemary, mint, and lavender favorites in your sachets and teas? Think of all the herbs and plants you love and use often, then begin researching their upkeep and care. Make sure to research your planting zone so you get the optimal climate to nurture your plants and herbs. Once you have planned your plantings, infuse your plot with magical intention. Keep careful track of your progress in your Book of Shadows. As you grow in experience and expertise, so will the healing power of your plot. Find out more about growing plants for healing in Chapter 3.

Remember to research plants and herbs that can be toxic or poisonous to ensure the safety of children or our canine and feline friends. Many a beloved power flower handed down to us is excellent for magical workings but not at all appropriate for tea, edibles, or such things. Make sure visiting children stay far away from wisteria, rhododendron, lily of the valley, narcissus, foxglove, larkspur, hydrangea, and oleander. They are beautiful but deadly, literally.

Every new moon is an opportunity to sow seeds for new beginnings and deepen your magical intent. Your plantings can be a tool you use for a better life, bringing brighter health and greater abundance, as well as mindfulness and serenity. Nature is our greatest teacher and a garden is a gift through which you both give and receive.

All the Seasons and Reasons for Altars

One of the most vital ways pagans can keep in touch with nature is through the creation of seasonal altars. Your altar helps you to maintain balance in your life and deepen your spiritual connection to the world around you. A seasonal altar is your tool for ceremonies to honor Mother Nature and receive the deep wisdom of the earth by blending the energies of shells, feathers, leaves, flowers, herbs, and all of the gifts of the season. Your periodic altars are the middle ground between Earth and sky, the meeting point of the four elements. Creating these altars is very life-affirming.

Spring

You can create a wonderful outdoor altar for spring by planning two seasons ahead and planting floral bulbs—flowers that are the very harbingers of spring such as tulips and lilies of the valley. When the bulbs begin to grow and bud, place an image or statue in the center of your altar, which could be a stone bench or the top of a rock wall. It could be a bust of a mythological youth to represent Hyacinth, immortalized in myth and in the gorgeous flower itself. Throughout the spring, you can stand inside your magic circle (see page 23) and pray and chant for the rebirth of nature that is spring.

Summer

During the season of sun and heat, the fullness of life and growth can be celebrated with the colors of yellow, green, and red. As you go on vacation, bring back shells and stones and create an altar devoted to this season of joy. As a card-carrying hearth witch, I have an outdoor fireplace, which is my seasonal shrine, and I adorn it with a lei of orchids, a spell bottle filled with sparkly golden sand, and gleaming shells from the beach. A yellow votive candle placed in a gorgeous opalescent abalone shell gently flames. An old brick imprinted with an image of the sun sits upright, standing guard over the humble shrine to the season of Helios.

Fall

Bring the bounty of the harvest to your kitchen altar. The leaves are falling and reaping-time is here. Now is the time for a gratitude altar reflecting the bounty and continuity of life. An arrangement of pumpkins, acorns, multicolored branches, and a handsome wreath will honor this time of abundance.

Winter

White and blue represent snow and sky. Star-shaped candles and a bare branch on your altar symbolize this time to go within, explore the inner reaches of self, and draw forth the insight for the coming spring. If you have a fireplace inside, this can be your altar for the coldest season, with candles burning to help create comfort and warmth.

CHAPTER 3

KITCHEN CUPBOARD HEALING

Herbs, Teas, and Curatives

A good witch knows that prevention is always better than a cure, and spellcraft can greatly assist the body's powerful self-healing properties. Healing spells are "earth magic"—a wonderful mix of gardening, herb lore, minding the moon and sky, and heeding ancient folk wisdom. Healing magic uses enchantments in conjunction with the properties of herbs and plants, meaning natural remedies can be found in your very own pantry and kitchen garden. The roses blooming by your front gate contain more vitamins than the expensive bottle of chemicals on your bathroom shelf. Your spice rack is your closest pharmacy. Inside your cupboard, a whole magical world awaits with which you can conjure much health and happiness.

The Homely Healing Arts

I began practicing the craft as a child. For me, witchcraft was and is the most natural thing in the world. On woodland walks, my Aunt Edith pointed out nettles, wild mint, Queen Anne's lace, and other herbs that grew by creek beds near my home. We picked, steeped, and sipped concoctions we made together as she imparted her homely wisdom. Little did I know at the time that I was being gently schooled as an apprentice kitchen witch.

We witches have to keep pace with the modern world, but our connection to the earth and the cycles of nature helps maintain balance and harmony, despite the hurly burly of these tech-driven times. This chapter is aimed at conjuring wellness so you can stay centered, grounded, and healthy. When our grandmothers and elders who came before us tended cuts, bruises, colds, fevers, and other illnesses their families suffered, they didn't have a corner drugstore. Instead, these wise women relied on simple wisdom, common sense, and pantries well stocked with herbal remedies. These preparations were made from plants that grew in the kitchen garden or from wild weeds gathered in the fields and woods surrounding their homes. This collection of kitchen-cupboard cures combines the wisdom of our elders with a modern kitchen witch's sensibilities. Yes, you will save money but, more importantly, you will begin to learn what works for you and master the art of self-care as you bring much comfort to your loved ones. Here are tips and witchy secrets to healing many maladies and feeling your best every day, come rain or shine.

Lavender Space-clearing Spell

To do any healing work, you must first clear clutter, both physical and otherwise, that creates energy blocks. Banish "stale" and unhealthy energy from your workspace and living space with this herbal magic. Steep lavender in hot water; once the infusion has cooled to room temperature, dip your fingertips in it and sprinkle tiny droplets throughout your home while intoning these words:

All is new here now, I say.
Make way, be gone, goodbye
All here is new, say I.
So mote it be!

Use the remainder of the lavender infusion to wash your front steps or stoop—the entry to your sanctuary—thereby clearing and cleansing the threshold of your home.

You will notice that every time you enter your home, it feels lighter and brighter thanks to the energetic decluttering.

Remedy Recipes

Many remedies can be made from what you have in the kitchen, from spices as well as herbs and plants. Here are a few simple tried-and-tested recipes handed down through generations of wise women:

* **Nutmeg Milk:** Grated nutmeg soothes heartburn, nausea, and upset tummies. Grate a small amount (about ⅛ teaspoon) to 1 mug of warmed milk (cow, soy, rice, or oat milk). It is comforting and curing.

* **Cayenne Infusion:** Use this pepper as a remedy for colds, coughs, sore throats, heartburn, hemorrhoids, and varicose veins, or as a digestive stimulant and to improve circulation. Make an infusion by adding ½ teaspoon cayenne powder to 1 cup (240ml) boiled water. Add 2 cups (480ml) of hot water to make a more pleasant and palatable infusion. Add lemon and honey to taste.

* **Catnip by the Cup:** This herb is not just for kitties! We humans can also benefit from it as a remedy for upset tummies as well as a way to diminish worry, anxiety, and nervous tension. Take a palmful of dried catnip leaves and steep in a cup (240ml) of boiling water for 5 minutes. Strain as you would any loose tea. Honey helps even more and a cup or two of catnip tea per day will have you in fine fettle, relaxed and ready.

* **Cranberry Cure:** How many times did your mom tell you to drink your cranberry juice? Turns out she was right to insist. Unsweetened cranberry juice is very good for bladder health and also benefits men as it's great for prostate health, too. Drink two half cups (two lots of 120ml) a day, mom's orders!

* **Echinacea Root:** Every herb store or organic grocer will have dried echinacea root for fighting colds and negating respiratory infections. It is an amazing immune booster! Just mince a teaspoonful and steep in a cup (240ml) of boiling water. Sweeten to taste and drink at least a couple of cups a day.

Other Herbs for Medicinal Teas

You can use the basic recipe of steeping a palmful of herbs for 5 minutes in a cup (240ml) of boiling water and use these plants either fresh or dried:

* **Lemon balm** is a true aid for insomnia, anxiety, and restlessness.

* **Licorice root** is marvelous for stomach and mouth ulcers.

* **Marshmallow**, both root and leaf, strengthens the gastrointestinal tract and your mucus membranes.

* **Milk thistle** is excellent for your liver and kidneys.

* **Mullein leaves** help sore throats, coughs, and chest congestion.

* **Nettle**, either fresh or dried, prevents allergies.

* **Slippery elm bark** will get rid of heartburn, a bad cough, and a sore throat.

* **St John's Wort** extract is good for depression, PMS, and hot flashes.

* **Thyme** is trusted to help with colds and congestion and is an antispasmodic.

The Spice Rack of Life

Did you know your pantry is like a pharmacy? Thankfully, it is far cheaper.

* **Cayenne** promotes circulation and boosts metabolism.

* **Turmeric** is an immune champion and boosts production of antioxidants and reduction of inflammation. Some centenarians have credited their long, healthy lives to drinking turmeric-root tea daily.

* **Cumin** is loaded with phytochemicals, antioxidants, iron, copper, calcium, potassium, manganese, selenium, zinc, and magnesium, and contains high amounts of B-complex. It also helps with insomnia.

* **Cilantro** (coriander) is a good source of iron, magnesium, phytonutrients, and flavonoids, and is also high in dietary fiber. Cilantro has been used for thousands of years as a digestive, helping lower blood sugar as it has hypoglycemic properties, possibly the result of helping to stimulate insulin secretion.

* **Parsley** is a nutrient-rich and detoxifying herb and acts as anti-inflammatory and anti-spasmodic, helping conditions from colic to indigestion. Rub it on itchy skin for instant relief.

* **Sage** is very beneficial in treating gum and throat infections. Sage tea has helped ease depression and anxiety for generations.

* **Ginger** stimulates circulation and is an excellent digestive, aiding in absorption of food and minimizing bloat.

* **Cinnamon** is a power spice. Just a half-teaspoon a day can dramatically reduce blood glucose levels in those with type 2 diabetes and help lower cholesterol.

* **Thyme** is a cure for hangover and doubles to alleviate colds and bronchitis.

* **Clove** is an antifungal and alleviates toothaches.

Pack your pantry with these seasonings for optimal health and happiness.

Breathe Easy Spell

10 drops rosemary

10 drops tea tree

10 drops eucalyptus

10 drops lavender

1 teaspoon sea salt

Banish colds and coughs or keep them at bay with this sweet-smelling spell. In a blue bottle, shake together the essential oils and salt.

Hold the open container in both hands under your nose and breathe in deeply three times. After the last exhalation, intone:

> *Power of wind,*
> *Strength of the trees,*
> *Energy of the earth,*
> *Salts of the sea,*
> *I call upon you to keep me well and strong.*
> *With harm to none, so mote it be.*

You can administer this respiratory booster with four drops added to the water of a vaporizer or diffuser or a cotton ball tucked into your pillowcase. Six drops poured into the running water of a hot bath will ease breathing immediately.

✳

ESSENTIAL OILS FOR COMMON AILMENTS

Use these oils in bath water, diffusers, dabbed onto pulse points, or sprays to infuse your home with the healing vitality of these plant essences.

Allergies: chamomile, melissa

Headaches: geranium, lavender, linden, peppermint

Immune boosters: hyssop, jasmine, rose, thyme

Insomnia: clary sage, hops, lavender

Colds and flu: eucalyptus, lavender, pine, thyme

Tummy troubles: basil, chamomile, peppermint

Cramps: linden, sunflower, yarrow

Arthritis: eucalyptus, marjoram, pine, rosemary

Fatigue: bergamot, clary sage, neroli, rose

First Aid Aromatherapy: Essential Oil Magic

Blending essential oils for magic is both an art and a science. Combining these herbal oils can take their individual properties to the next level, interacting together to perform curative miracles.

Classic Essential Oils

* One drop of lavender essential oil warmed between the palms of your hands can summon an instant sense of serenity.

* One whiff of bergamot essential oil can calm anxiety and stimulate the mind.

* Ylang ylang essential oil can combat hypertension.

* Rosemary essential oil kindles the memory and can help with perspiration.

A great blend involves combining notes—typically a top, middle, and base, although some blends don't require a base—to create a balanced and effective aroma.

The top note is the first scent impression, which gives way to the middle note—the star of the show. The base note gives the blend its staying power and usually comes to the forefront much later. The aim in blending these three notes is to create a ratio that results in a harmonious cocktail that works (olfactorily or topically, depending on the blend) to address specific moods or ailments. A good rule of thumb is to use approximately 30 percent top note, 50 percent middle, and 20 percent base. If the blend doesn't require a base note, round it up to about 40 percent top and 60 percent middle. Always use the highest-quality organic essential oils (see Resources, page 205) for the best outcomes. Consult your local herbal apothecary and look for brands that have had GC/MS testing as that is known as the gold standard test for essential oils. I keep a stock of ½-ounce (15ml) dark-colored vials with stopper lids and blank labels for when aromatherapy needs arise.

For the following blends, carefully pour the oils into a vial and shake gently to blend. You can rub this on pulse points or use a diffuser. These are quite popular. If you are using a diffuser, no carrier (or base) oil is needed. I use the simplest and most old-fashioned kind of diffuser, which is a clay ring you can put at the base of a light bulb in a lamp. The warmth of the bulb slowly fills the space with the desired scent and effect. If you plan to use your blend on pulse points, you will need a carrier oil. Always do a skin test first to avoid any potential irritation.

Jubilant

The sweet scent of this blend makes you feel all warm and fuzzy—euphoric, even.

1 drop each of top notes: bergamot, lemon, neroli

1 drop each of middle notes: ylang ylang, jasmine, Roman chamomile, geranium, rose

1 tablespoon of a carrier (or base) oil, ideally jojoba or apricot

Quietude

If you need a moment of peace, try this citrus-floral blend.

3 drops of top note: orange

5 drops of middle note: ylang ylang

2 drops of base note: patchouli

1 teaspoon carrier (or base) oil, ideally sesame or jojoba

Bright Mind

Clear the mind and gain a keen sense of alertness with this bright, sunny blend.

1 drop each of top notes: rosemary, peppermint, bergamot, lemon

1 drop each of middle notes: mint, geranium, ylang ylang, jasmine, Roman chamomile

1 teaspoon carrier (or base) oil, almond or grapeseed

Dandy Sassafras Ginger Detox

✳ DECOCTIONS 101

Roots, bark, and herbs with tough stems and seeds don't really lend themselves to the method of infusing. Decocting is boiling and then evaporating by simmering slowly to produce the most concentrated liquid, which is excellent in medicines. Use a coffee grinder for roots and small pieces of bark and stems to make quick work of these. I recommend the decoction method for the roots of willow, sarsaparilla, wild cherry, yohimbe, yucca, licorice, parsley, dandelion, angelica, and cohosh.

When I was little, living on the family farm, I accompanied my part-Cherokee dad to the woods, looking for sassafras roots to make tea. I loved the taste; it was delightful and also gave me more energy. After apprenticing with my dad for a few years, he allowed me to go out alone, gathering the source of my dearly beloved beverage. Years later, I discovered that sassafras was highly prized by Native Americans who used it for medicine and who were extremely knowledgeable about combining herbs to amplify their power.

This morning-medicine is inspired by a shamanic native-healing recipe using sassafras roots, dandelion greens, and slices of wild ginger. For a wonderfully medicinal decoction, take a half-cup of each and boil them in spring water. After steeping for 12 minutes, stir in honey and enjoy. It is pleasantly surprising how good the detox tastes and even more how the herbs combine to eliminate toxins from the body, chiefly the kidney and liver. During the holidays or pagan-feast times, we all imbibe and enjoy rich foods, good wine, and sugary desserts. This purifying herbal blend will cleanse the organs that cleanse your body, thus aiding wellness. This detox should be used seasonally and is not intended for daily use, due to its great power.

Oxymel: An Ancient Tonic

Oxymel is a very old-fashioned tonic that dates back to ancient times and that has fallen out of fashion. It remains a favorite of herbal healers and is made of two seemingly opposing ingredients—honey and vinegar. Herbs can be added to great effect and when you see honey-menthol cough drops on the pharmacy shelf, note their 2,000-year-old origins. Oxymels are supremely effective for respiratory issues. The recipe is simplicity itself, equal parts honey and vinegar poured over herbs in a canning jar. Store in a dark cupboard and give the sealed jar a good shake every day. After two weeks, strain out the herbs through cheesecloth and store in the fridge.

*
HERBS FOR OXYMELS

The herbs that I would recommend using for this healing tonic are oregano, elder flower, sage, balm, mint, lemon peel, thyme, lavender, rose petals, hyssop, and fennel.

Blackberries: Roadside Medicine

Blackberries are one of life's sweetest gifts, growing abundantly in the bramble along many a rambling path. An extremely effective medicinal tonic can be made by soaking 4 cups (520g) of berries in a quart (1 liter) of malt vinegar for three days. Drain and strain the liquid into a pan. Simmer and stir in sugar, 2¼ cups (450g) to every 2 cups (480ml) of tonic. Boil gently for 5 minutes and skim off any foam. Cool and pour into a sealable jar.

This potion is so powerful that you can add a teaspoon into a cup of water and cure tummy aches, cramps, fevers, coughs, and colds. Best of all, blackberry vinegar is both a medicine and a highly prized culinary flavoring for sauces and salads. Pour some over your apple pie and cream and you will soon scurry off to pick blackberries all summer.

Comfrey Comfort

Comfrey is beloved by kitchen witches and is one of the best-known healing herbs of all times. It has even been referred to as "a one-herb pharmacy" for its inherent curative powers. Well known and widely used by early Greeks and Romans, its botanical name, *symphytum*, from the Greek *symphyo*, means to "make grow together," referring to its traditional use of healing fractures. Comfrey relieves pain and inflammation. Comfrey salve will be a mainstay of your home first-aid kit. Use it on cuts, scrapes, rashes, sunburn, and almost any skin irritation. Comfrey salve can also bring comfort to aching arthritic joints and sore muscles.

Lavender Comfrey Cure-all Salve

¾ cup (180ml) comfrey-infused oil

¼ cup (60ml) coconut oil

4 tablespoons beeswax

10 drops lavender essential oil

Combine the comfrey and coconut oils. Heat the oil and wax together until the wax melts completely. Pour into a clean, dry jar. When the mixture has cooled a little, but not yet set, add 10 drops of lavender essential oil, which is also an antiseptic. Stir it through. Seal the jar and store in a cabinet to use anytime you scratch yourself working in the garden or want to renew and soften your hands and feet after a lot of house and yard work. One note, use it on the outside of your skin and it will work wonders, but if a cut is deep, don't get it inside the wound. Let your physician handle that. Comfrey is a miracle plant for healing; in combination with the lavender, this power duo will restore your spirit along with your skin.

Heart's Ease Cauldron Cure

Here is a soothing sip that can uplift your spirits anytime and also serves to ward off chills. This combination of herbs brings about the "letting go" of sorrows, worries, and doubts, and reignites feelings of self-love.

Stir all the ingredients together in a clean cauldron to mix. Pour into a colored jar, and seal the lid tightly. When you are ready to brew, pour hot water over the herbs, two teaspoons per cup. While this steeps for 5 minutes, write down on a small piece of paper any thoughts or fears of which you need to rid yourself. Now say each one aloud, then chant, "Begone!" After this letting-go ritual, burn the paper together with sage in the cauldron on your altar. As you sip the tea, enjoy your renewed sense of self and peace of mind.

1 ounce (28g) dried rosehips
1 ounce (28g) dried hibiscus
2 ounces (56g) dried mint
1 tablespoon dried ginger root

✳ MOTHER NATURE'S MULTIVITAMIN

Once a rose has bloomed and all petals have fallen away, the hip is ready to be picked. Ground rose hips are the best source of immune-boosting Vitamin C; they contain 50 percent more Vitamin C than oranges. One tablespoon provides more than the recommended daily adult allowance of 90 mg for men and 75 mg for women. The pulp from rose hips may be used in sauces or made into jelly. What a delicious way to ward off colds and ailments!

Luxuriating in Lavender

Lavender is prized for its lovely scent and is a powerful healing plant with other properties, too. It can be used for making teas, as well as having many more practical uses. For tea, the rule of thumb is one teaspoon dried lavender flowers to one cup (240ml) boiling water to aid tummy trouble, headache, aches, insomnia, and even to help calming the mind. You can easily amp up the therapeutic power of your brew by adding any of these excellent herbs—dried yarrow, St. John's wort, or chamomile.

This is a simple and streamlined way to infuse lavender: pour a heaping tablespoon into a bowl of hot water and then drape a towel over your head and breathe in the aromatic fumes to deal with respiratory issues, coughs, colds, headaches, stuffy sinuses, and nervous tension. You will come away feeling renewed and your kitchen will smell like the heavens above. You can use the water in your morning bath or add to your sink garbage disposal; grinding up the flowers refreshes that hard-duty kitchen appliance.

Lavender Tincture

Clear quart jar with lid

Dried lavender

1 cup (240ml) clear alcohol, such as vodka

2 cups (480ml) distilled water

Cheesecloth

Dark glass for storage

This cure-all should be kept on hand at all times for soothing the skin, the stomach, and anything in need of comfort. I have even seen it used to staunch bleeding in small cuts.

Fill your clear quart jar to the halfway point with the dried lavender. Pour in the alcohol also to the halfway point. Add in the water, seal securely with a lid, and shake for a few minutes until it seems well mixed. Store in a dark cupboard for one month, shaking once a day. After 30 days, strain through the cheesecloth into the dark glass storage jar and screw the lid on tightly. The lavender leavings will make lovely compost and the liquid tincture will soon prove itself indispensible in your household.

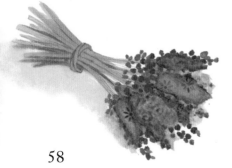

Easy Apple Cider Vinegar

Apple cider vinegar can be used in your cookery, as a daily health drink, household cleanser, skin and facial toner, a hair rinse, and for dozens of other excellent applications. It lowers cholesterol and blood pressure and helps strengthen bones; best of all, it costs mere pennies to make as you are only using the cores and peels from the apples. Bake a couple of pies while you brew up a tonic health booster.

Cut up the apple cores and peels into smaller pieces and spoon into a wide-mouthed canning jar. Pour in the water to cover the fruit, spoon in the honey, and stir well. Cover the mixture with a clean paper towel or waxed paper and place a rubber band tightly around the neck of the jar. Place on a dark shelf in your cupboard or work area and leave for two weeks. Strain the liquid and remove the compostable solids that remain, return the liquid to the jar and secure the paper and band again. Put it back on the shelf and make sure to stir daily. After one month, take a spoonful and if the acidity and flavor is to your taste, transfer to a dark bottle with sealable top. If not, wait another week and then taste it again. Vinegar will corrode metal lids so a pretty bottle with a cork is the best option.

8 organic apple cores and peels

1 quart (1 liter) water

2 tablespoons honey

DIY Herbal Vinegar

When you add herbs to vinegar, you are enhancing the healing power of the best of both worlds. Many herbs make for excellent vinegars (see right), so pay attention to which ones are especially appealing to you as you go about your gardening. The more herbs you pack into the jar, the higher the mineral content in your vinegar, which makes it more flavorful and healthy. Once you have your own apple cider vinegar or a premade organic kind, pick an herb you know works for you and pack a quart canning jar as full as you can with it. Pour room-temperature apple cider vinegar to cover and seal with paper and bands and pop back on a dark corner shelf for six weeks, giving it a shake once a week. At the end of the infusion period, strain out any remaining compostable twigs or stems that remain, if any, store in a colored bottle, and add a pretty label.

✳

HERBAL ALCHEMY

The leaves and stalks of these plants are very good for making herbal vinegars: apple mint, basil, catnip, garlic mustard, orange mint, peppermint, rosemary, spearmint, thyme, and yarrow. Dill and fennel seeds work very well as do lemon and orange peels. The flowers of bee balm, chives, goldenrod, lavender, and yarrow produce a great flavor.

Roots also infuse nicely into herbal vinegars—the best are dandelion, chicory, ginger, garlic, mugwort, and burdock.

A Mug of Magic

The British and kitchen witches have one thing in common—they believe a good pot of tea can fix almost anything. And it is true—heartache, headaches, and all manner of ills seem to evaporate in the steam that rises from the spout of the kettle. With a handful of herbs and a cauldron-full of witchy wisdom, big healing can result from a small cup of tea.

Once you have the knack of making tea, you can also brew up simples, digestives, tisanes, tonics, tinctures, and the many other concoctions that can be created right at home. This is one of the most delightful aspects of kitchen witchery as these recipes are usually easy enough as long as you have the proper ingredients. They make all the difference after a long day at the office; they can be enjoyed alone and can also be shared to great effect. When bottled and hand labeled, these potions can also make significant gifts that will be long remembered for the thoughtfulness as well as the delight and comfort received. Prepare to brew up much joy.

Simply Yarrow

Teas brewed from a single herb are commonly called simples, a lovely phrase from olden times. Experience has taught me that simples often have the most potency; the purity of that single plant essence can come through undiluted. This book contains a plentitude of herbs you can use to brew tasty, helpful, and healing simples, but yarrow is one you should brew regularly. Boil 2½ cups (600ml) of spring water. Place a half-ounce (15ml) of dried yarrow into your favorite crockery pot and pour over the water. Steep for 10 minutes and strain with a non-metallic implement, such as an inexpensive bamboo strainer or cheesecloth. Sweeten with honey; clover honey intensifies the positivity of this potion and makes it a supremely lucky drink. Yarrow brings courage, heart, and is a major medicine. All these aspects make yarrow one of the most strengthening of all simples.

Jasmine Joy Ritual

Jasmine tea is a delightful concoction and can create an aura of bliss and conviviality. It is available at any grocer or purveyor of organic goods, but homegrown is even better. Brew a cup of jasmine tea and let it cool. Add two parts lemonade to one part jasmine tea and drink the mixture with a good friend. Jasmine is a vine and represents the intertwining of people. You will be more bonded to anyone with whom you share this sweet ritual.

This is also a tonic that you can indulge in when alone. I recommend brewing up a batch every Monday, or "Moon Day," to ensure that each week is filled with joyfulness.

As the jasmine tea steeps, pray:

On this Moon Day in this new week,
I call upon the spirits to guide joy to my door.
By this moon on this day, I call upon Selene, goddess fair
To show me the best way to live.
For this, I am grateful.
Blessed be the brew; blessed be me.

✳
TELEPATHY TEA

The humble dandelion, abhorred by lawn keepers everywhere, hides its might very well. Dandelion root tea can call upon the spirit of anyone whose advice you might need. Simply place a freshly brewed simple using this herbal root on your bedroom altar or nightstand. Before you sleep, say the name of your helper aloud seven times. In a dream or vision, the spirit will visit you and answer all your questions. During medieval times, this spell was used to find hidden treasure. Chaucer, who was well-versed in astrology and other metaphysics, advised this tried and true tea.

Pantry Power

Many enthusiasts enjoy several cups a day of their favorite herbal infusion, which is a large portion of herb brewed for at least four hours and as long as ten. I recommend one cup of the dried herb placed in a quart-canning jar and filled with freshly boiled water. After the steeping, strain using a non-metallic method, such as cheesecloth or bamboo. Herbal infusions can be made with the leaves and fruits that provide the magical and healing aspects of this comforting concoction. Many of the favorite kitchen witch herbs contain minerals, antioxidants, and phytochemicals. Roots, leaves, flowers, needles, and seeds can all be used—depending on which fruit or herb is chosen to be the base. There are some cases when all parts of the plant can be used in some manner, and for others only one or two parts are safe—it is important, when creating a blend from scratch, to research the ingredients to understand what parts can be used.

What do you need to attend to in your life right now? This list of herbs and associations can be your guide; one of the smartest ways to approach this methodology is to brew right before bedtime and you will awaken to a freshly infused herb. Opposite I've listed some of the most popular herbs and fruits used to create infusions.

✳

BLESSINGS ON A BUDGET

Instead of composting all the herbs, twigs, and stems from your brews, you can store them in a burlap or muslin sack and allow them to dry. Keep stuffing in twigs of lavender, rosemary, mint, and all the leftover plant material until you have a big bag. On a special evening, burn it in your fireplace or an outdoor bonfire and it will be like a gigantic incense burner with lovely scents wafting from the flames. And the best part? It's one hundred percent free!

* **Anise seeds and leaves** soothe cramps and aches

* **Caraway seeds** aid in romantic issues and help with colic

* **Catnip leaves** increase attractiveness

* **Chamomile flowers** help with sleep and are good for abundance

* **Dandelion leaves** make wishes come true

* **Echinacea** makes the body strong

* **Ginseng root** increases men's vigor

* **Nettle leaves** are good for lung function and hex breaking

* **Peppermint leaves** rid tummy discomfort and are cleansing

* **Pine needles** increase skin health as well as financial health

* **Rose hip fruit** is packed with Vitamin C and can halt colds and flu

* **Sage leaves** purify energy and are a natural antibiotic

* **Skullcap leaves** cure insomnia, headaches, anxiety, and nervous tension

* **St.-John's-wort leaves** act as an anti-depressant and provide protection

* **Thyme leaves** are antiseptic and a protectant

* **Yarrow flowers** reduce fever and bring courage and good luck

A Cup Brimming with Health: Vitamin C Tea

This tonic provides bioflavonoids and vitamin C in an organic, natural way so all the nutrients are easily available for absorption. Drink this blend regularly and you will feel fantastic. The amounts of ingredients are given in parts, as you may want to make a big batch of tea for the whole family.

2 parts lemongrass

3 parts hibiscus

4 parts rose hips

1 part chopped cinnamon sticks

A teapot

Honey

Blend the herbs using your mortar and pestle. Place in a teapot with 4 cups (960ml) of hot water. Steep for 5 minutes in your teapot, then strain and serve sweetened with honey to taste. If you make ahead, you should keep the mixed herbs in an airtight container. Serve regularly as a preventative during cold and flu season.

Quick Tips: BLACK, GREEN, AND WHITE TEA

Use black tea for an upset tummy and headache. Green tea strengthens the immune system, and you can reuse tea bags to stanch cuts or calm insect bites. White tea, green tea, and black tea are all made from the leaves of *Camellia sinensis*. White tea is made from the youngest leaves of the plant; it is a sweet brew and has less caffeine than green or black tea. It is also rich in antioxidants and is recommended for reducing "bad" cholesterol and improving artery health. White tea is a little costly, but a good choice for health and flavor.

A Garden of Health and Healing

I have already mentioned the healing properties of various herbs; herein, I have gathered the plants, flowers, and herbs that I suggest you grow yourself, as they will prove most useful in your kitchen witchery. Most are hardy plants that you and your circle will enjoy for many long years to come and that will bring both beauty and power to your garden.

Thyme—An Herb for the Ages

You could say that thyme is a classic herb, so much so that the venerable Virgil and Pliny sang the praises of this medicinal mint relative over 2,000 years ago. While thyme loves Mediterranean weather, it can grow elsewhere from seeds and cuttings. Good for the stomach and especially effective for respiratory relief, thyme induces sweats to remove toxins and reduce fever. Thyme honey tea is truly a sweet way to make the medicine go down, so much so that you will drink it even when hale and hearty. Thyme is also a culinary plant, making a delightful additive to savory dishes. When I lived in warmer climes, I planted wooly thyme among the flagstones of my front yard and let it spread as

much as possible. When I came home from work, the sunny, 80-plus-degree weather had warmed the thyme, creating a perfumed walkway. Arriving home was a heavenly experience.

It has been believed for centuries that thyme brings courage and both inner and physical strength. Even when you are facing seemingly insurmountable odds, spells and smudging featuring thyme can get you on track and bring you to your goal. I think the greatest of all aspects of thyme is to rid your home and family of melancholy and overcome despair after extreme difficulty and loss. If your loved ones have experienced a catastrophe, try thyme for rituals of magic and restitution. I have no doubt that practitioners of green witchery will be singing the praises of thyme for at least 2,000 more years.

✳

DREAM THYME

I gather and dry thyme to use in sachets so the divine fragrance freshens linens and laundry. A little bag of this dried thyme tucked in your pillowcase makes for sweeter sleep. As if all that wasn't enough, it also repels bugs and pests but attracts honeybees!

Balm for All Sorrows

Lemon balm also goes by the equally lovely Latinate *Melissa*. From Greco-Roman times, this relative of the mint family has been held as a significant medicine. You can grow lemon balm with ease from seed packets in almost any kind of soil, but it likes shade in the afternoon to prevent wilting. This is one of the happy plants that will "volunteer" and spread in your garden and can be used in love magic—to bring love to you and heal after a break up or divorce. It can also be employed as an aphrodisiac.

Infusions and teas made from lemon balm make good on the offer the name implies—it can soothe the heart and any lingering upset, blue moods, and aches and pains from trauma, both physical and emotional. We should all grow as much as possible and let some of it go to seed for those new plants that will pop up in unexpected places in your herb garden. A kitchen witch never complains about a plentitude of balm; anyone who makes much use of lemon balm in brews and cookery will enjoy an abundance of love.

Chives for Good Cheer

Allium, also known as chives, is a blessedly easy plant to grow anywhere and everywhere—on the kitchen windowsill or in a garden patch. A member of the onion family, this is a lovely case where the entire plant—bulb, leaves, and flowers—can be eaten. Plant the bulbs 6 inches (15 cm) apart, water, and you can pretty much ignore them after as all they require is water. A plus is that this relative of the onion has insect-repellant properties, so you can plant rows of this beside veggies and fruits and the bugs will stay away. Allium propagates quickly, so you can dig up mature bulbs and separate them and replant. One tip to remember is that chives do lose their flavor when dried, so use them fresh.

The flowers are a lovely surprise to add to salads for their edible beauty and many a kitchen witch uses chives in all manner of dishes as it is good for weight management and is a plant of protection for both home and garden. Chives were used by practitioners of old in amulets to ward off evil spirits and mischievous fairy folk. Freshly cut bunches were also hung beside the sickbed to speed healing, especially for children. If you see a home surrounded by rows of allium, you know its occupants hold to the "old ways."

Basil: Bounty and Beauty

This sweet-tasting herb is excellent in savory dishes. Basil truly grows like a weed and you should cultivate it right on the kitchen windowsill so you can snip and add to your Italian-inspired dishes. Give your basil plants plenty of sun, lots of water, and you will reap a mighty bounty to share with the neighbors. Old wives and hedge witches claim that basil protects your home while it also brings prosperity and happiness. Basil helps steady the mind, brings love, peace, and money, and protects against insanity—what more can you want? Basil has many practical magical applications such as making peace after disagreements. The benefits of this plant are as plentiful as the plant itself; it can be used in attracting and getting love and, on the highest vibrational level, abetting psychic abilities, even astral projection.

Basil Money Magic

Harvest several leaves from your basil plants and place them inside a clear bowl of water on your kitchen altar overnight. In the morning, remove the leaves and let them dry on your kitchen windowsill. Touch the water to your fingertips and touch your purse, wallet, and anywhere you keep money. If you handle money at your workplace, bottle some of the basil water in a tiny jar and do the same. Once the soaked leaves have dried, place one in your wallet, purse, and pockets to attract money to you and yours. It also repels thieves and protects from a loss of wealth. You can also put some basil leaves on your desk at home or work to enhance prosperity for your employer or before asking for a raise. Basil is truly a kitchen witch's boon.

*

EDIBLE FLOWERS

Organic, pesticide-free posies are tasty additions to salads, cake décor, and even savories, such as fried squash blossom. Flowers add a stunning beauty to any dish. Grab your basket and add a bouquet to your culinary creations: impatiens, marigold, gladiola, daylily, cornflower, daisy, carnation, and viola. My favorites are peppery, fresh-flavored nasturtiums, which are so easy to grow and the yellow, red and, bright-orange blooms are the colors of happiness.

Daisy and Echinacea

This faithful flower's name is derived from the Anglo-Saxon *dæges eage*, "day's eye," since it closes in the evening. The daisy has been used in one of the oldest of love charms. To know if your true love is returned, take a daisy and intone, "He loves me, he loves me not" until the last petal is plucked and the answer will be revealed. This flower is not just a boon for romance, however, it is also useful in herbal medicine for aches, bruises, wounds, inflammation, and soothing eye baths. As a flower remedy, it is quite good to help with exhaustion and is a highly regarded cure in homeopathy.

Echinacea is a member of the daisy family that has become wildly popular as a healer for colds and as a powerful immune booster, increasing your T-cell count and fighting off illnesses both minor and major. Echinacea is an herb of abundance, attracting more prosperity, but it can be used in magic workings to amplify the power of spellwork.

Rosemary for Remembrance

Rosemary is another of the herbs that thrives best in warm, Mediterranean climes but can also weather the cold. Tough to grow from seed, cuttings are an easier way to start your row of rosemary plants in your garden. Pots of this bushy plant can enjoy spring and summer and come in from the cold to a sheltered porch or by a sunny window when temperatures drop. As a bonus, it requires little water. Rosemary is fantastic as a seasoning for potatoes, roast chicken, and makes any Sunday supper taste better and brighter. You can pinch off the aromatic needles to dress plates or sprinkle into soups and stews. Beyond enhancing your cookery, this is a primary plant for rejuvenation and is prized for how it helps restore after lingering illness; elixirs and essential oils made from rosemary stimulate and energize as they comfort.

In Greco-Roman times, rosemary was believed to help the memory. An excellent kitchen witchery practice is to take dried or fresh rosemary and add it to a steam for an easy infusion, where it aids breathing, muscle aches, and anxiety. You can accomplish the same by adding rosemary to a hot bath. Lie back and relax, remembering happy times in your life, and those that lie right ahead of you.

Coltsfoot: Dispeller of Coughs

Coltsfoot, also called butterbur, is so named for the leaf's resemblance to a horse's hoof. Viewed as a weed except for those who know, this spiky, flowering plant grows wild along creeks, wetlands, or loamy fields. *Tussilago*, the Latinate botanical name, means cough dispeller, and this is a powerful aid to those with asthma or bronchial conditions and is also very good medicine for colds and flu. In folklore, young maidens would use the leaves in a simple spell to see their future husband in the distance, galloping toward them. Truly knowledgeable hedge witches have a herd of coltsfoot in the shadiest, dampest part of their property.

Angelica: Heavenly Guardian Flower

Angelica, said to bloom first on Archangel Michael's name day, is part of the carrot family and is a tall, hollow-stemmed plant with umbrella-shaped clusters of pale, white flowers, tinged with green. Candying the stalks in sugar was an old-fashioned favorite; it was also traditionally used to cure colds and relieve coughs. Nowadays, seeds are used to make chartreuse, a digestif and uniquely tasty liqueur. This guardian flower is a protector, as one might expect from a plant associated with archangels, and is used to reverse curses, break hexes, and fend off negative energies. Drying and curing the root makes for a traditional talisman, which can be carried in your pocket or in an amulet to bring long life. Many a wise woman has used angelica leaves in baths and spellwork to rid a household of dark spirits. If the bad energy is intense, burn the angelica leaves with frankincense to exorcise them from your space. While you are protecting yourself and your home from negativity during this angelica smudging session, you will also experience heightened psychism. Pay close attention to your dreams after this; important messages will come through.

Lavender is Love

Lavender is blessedly easy to grow as it is a shrubby plant of Mediterranean origins. Once your seedlings and young plants have been established, they will bush out and produce loads of scented stalks, flowers, and seeds. This bounty will become your source for teas, tinctures, bath salts, and infusions. It can even prosper in dry and droughty areas, so make sure your kitchen garden has at least one of the hardy varieties so you can dry bundles to use in your spellwork as well as in your recipes.

Lavender Self-blessing Ritual

The time you take to restore yourself is precious. Morning is the optimal time to perform a self-blessing, which will help you maintain your physical health and provide an emotional boost each and every day. Take a bundle of dried lavender grown in your kitchen garden or from a purveyor of organic herbs and place it into a muslin sack. Knead the lavender three times and breathe in the calming scent. Beginning at the top of your head, your crown chakra, pass the pouch all the way down to your feet, gently touching your other six sacred chakras: your forehead, throat, solar plexus, upper and lower abdomen, and pelvis. Holding the lavender bag over your heart, speak aloud the spell on the right.

Gone are sorrows, illness, and woe;
Here wisdom and health flows.
My heart is whole, joy fills my soul.
Blessed be me.

Sage Wisdom

Every kitchen witch should grow a pot of sage or a big patch in her garden. Sage is a must to have on hand for clearing energy. It also increases psychic potential. Most kitchen witches are highly imaginative and very inventive folk. Whether your passion is growing an artful garden, throwing pots, cookery, or music, you can stay in better touch with your personal muse. Call her to you anytime, day or night, by your own design. This is especially important if you are feeling uninspired or struggling with a bout of writer's block.

Head out to your garden or the sunny spot on the deck where your hardiest sage grows. Take three large and extra-long sticks of your favorite incense and bind strands of sage around the incense with purple thread. Tie it off and you have a sage wand. Before any creative endeavor, you can light this wand and wave it around your workspace, filling the area with inspiration. Close your eyes and meditate upon the work you will begin. You have cleared your space, invited the muse, and your work will be superb, worthy of notice from the gods and goddesses.

✳

PLANTING PROTECTION

Plants provide a haven, even in a small studio apartment. They lend their seasonal beauty to any environment, whether at home or at work.

Did you know that plants can also improve the air we breathe? They purify the air by producing oxygen and absorbing contaminants, like formaldehyde and benzene, which are commonly off-gassed by furniture and mattresses. Try keeping bamboo, weeping fig, rubber tree, spider plant, peace lily, or snake plant.

Houseplants need their leaves dusted and you can do this with a banana peel. The dust clings to the peel and the leaves are nourished by it. Go bananas!

Aloe: Medicine Tree

One of Mother Nature's most effective healers is aloe. When I lived in colder areas of frost and snow, I grew aloe in a wide pot with good drainage and placed it in the sunniest spot in the kitchen, where it thrived with very little water. I am truly fortunate to live today where it never gets below freezing, so I have a towering aloe in the left garden corner that is growing to tree-like proportion. When anyone in the household gets a burn, a bug bite, a rash, a scratch, an itch, or sunburn, I march back and grab a stem and apply the juice liberally to the affected area. We use it as a medicine and as a beauty application for facials, hair gel, skin massage, and feel so blessed that all this heavenly healing is utterly free of cost. Aloe propagates through baby plants sprouting off the sides, which you can repot into little clay containers and give as kitchen witchery gifts to your circle to share the healing energy as well as protection and luck, a deterrent to loneliness and to help abet success. Grow in the home to provide protection from household accidents. Burn on the night of a full moon to bring a new lover by the new moon.

Mint: Refresh Your Mental Powers

Another useful herb is mint, which is so easily grown that a little bunch in the backyard can go on to become a scented, attractive groundcover. It is also called the flower of eternal refreshment. Woven into a laurel, it bestows brilliance, artistic inspiration, and prophetic ability. As a tea, it accomplishes miracles of calming the stomach and the mind at the same time.

Astrological Almanac of Green Witchery

Plants carry potent energy you can use to amplify your magical workings. Use the signs of the Sun, Moon, and stars to your advantage and, over time, you will come to know which ones are most effective for you. Make sure to use your own astrological chart in working with these herbs.

Here is a guide to the astrological associations of plants you may be growing in your kitchen garden or keep dried in your pantry:

* **Aries**, ruled by Mars: carnation, cedar wood, clove, cumin, fennel, juniper, peppermint, and pine

* **Taurus**, ruled by Venus: apple, daisy, lilac, magnolia, oak moss, orchid, plumeria (frangipani), rose, thyme, tonka bean, vanilla, and violet

* **Gemini**, ruled by Mercury: almond, bergamot, clover, dill, lavender, lemongrass, lily, mint, and parsley

* **Cancer**, ruled by the Moon: eucalyptus, gardenia, jasmine, lemon, lotus, myrrh, rose, and sandalwood

* **Leo**, ruled by the Sun: acacia, cinnamon, heliotrope, nutmeg, orange, and rosemary

* **Virgo**, ruled by Mercury: almond, cypress, bergamot, mace, mint, moss, patchouli, and thyme

* **Libra**, ruled by Venus: catnip, marjoram, mugwort, spearmint, sweet pea, thyme, and vanilla

* **Scorpio**, ruled by Pluto: allspice, basil, cumin, galangal, and ginger

* **Sagittarius**, ruled by Jupiter: anise, cedar wood, honeysuckle, sassafras, and star anise

* **Capricorn**, ruled by Saturn: lemon thyme, mimosa, vervain, and vetiver

* **Aquarius**, ruled by Uranus: citron, cypress, gum, lavender, pine, and spearmint

* **Pisces**, ruled by Neptune: clover, neroli, orris, sarsaparilla, and sweet pea

Mineral Medicine

Since the dawn of human kind, people have carried stones and crystals as helpers and as talismans; for protection and good luck. In so doing, they have brought themselves a greater sense of security. For peace of mind, the strongest "medicine" consists of an amethyst, a rhodochrosite, and a turquoise. While they may sound exotic, they are commonly available in metaphysical stores.

A small sky-blue bag

An amethyst crystal

A rhodochrosite crystal

A turquoise crystal

Place the crystals in the bag. When you are ready, hold the pouch in your hand and incant:

Stones of the earth, warmed by the sun,
Clear away trouble,
Help and healing is now begun.

I recommend leaving your pouch on your altar where it can be at the ready whenever needed.

Awesome Altar Stones

Crystals are finally being acknowledged for their power to give greater physical strength and health, and can be added to your healing altar (see page 78). Turquoise stones are grounding, and agates raise the energy level. For good circulation, try carnelian. For keeping life on an even keel, the organic gem family—shells, corals, and abalone—is optimal. For impetus and motivation, work with carnelian. To boost your health and well-being, try red coral for the lungs, bloodstone for the heart, and moonstone during pregnancy.

Quick Tips: INSTANT INSPIRATION

* To lift your spirits, light a green candle and hold harmony-bringing jade while meditating.

* Carrying a quartz crystal will create tranquility inside and around you.

* If you're feeling overwhelmed or under duress, hold black obsidian. If the stress is caused by an overabundant workload, keep the obsidian on your desk. Obsidian absorbs the negative.

The Goddess of Healing: Artemis Invocation

Creating a healing altar will safeguard your physical health and that of your loved ones. Your altar is your sacred workspace. It is charged with your personal power. Set up your healing altar facing north, the direction associated with the energy of manifestation. North is also the direction of the hour of midnight, the "witching hour," and an altar set up facing north at midnight promises potent magic. Your shrine to the healing craft should be highly personal and represent all that signifies wellness to you.

This altar is dedicated to the goddess Artemis (see right).

White fabric

2 green candles, for health, in green glass holders or votive glasses

A small statue of Artemis, or a moon-shaped symbol to represent her

Incense such as sandalwood, camphor, or frankincense

Healing crystals and objects that bring comfort

To ensure healthful beginnings, drape the white fabric over your altar to make a tabula rasa, or altar equivalent to a blank slate. Take the candles and position them in the two farthest corners of the altar. Place the Artemis statue at the center of the altar. Place an incense burner between the two candles and light the incense.

Now adorn your altar with objects that symbolize healing energy to you. You may perhaps choose a candleholder carved from a chunk of amethyst crystal, which contains healing properties; an abalone shell with the iridescent magic of the oceans; a sweet-smelling bundle of sage; a small citrus plant bursting with the restorative power of vitamins; or a bowl of curative salts from the sea.

These symbolic items, and any others that you select, will energize your altar with the magic that lives inside you. It is also important that the altar be pleasing to your eye and makes you feel good when you look at it so that you want to spend time there each and every day. After you have been performing rituals there for a while, a positive healing energy field will radiate from your altar.

Artemis, Goddess of the Healing Moon

Artemis is one of the best-known goddesses and, as it turns out, is one of the most needed as she is a healing divinity. She is the Greek goddess of the moon. In her Roman form, Diana, she is the deity to whom Dianic witches and priestesses are devoted. She is a bringer of luck, the goddess of the hunt, and a powerful deity for magic and spellwork. As the huntress, she can help you search out anything you are looking for, whether it is tangible or intangible. As a lunar deity, she can illuminate you. Invoke Artemis when you want to practice moon magic, by saying aloud "I call upon you, beloved Artemis." I suggest you study her mythology further to design original lunar ceremonies. Enshrine her by dedicating an altar or sacred space to her to bring about any of her marvelous qualities and to bring about healing.

Quick Tip: EARRING ALLEVIATION

Wear one gold earring and one silver earring to rid yourself of the discomfort of a headache.

CHAPTER 4

NURTURING LOVE

Romance, Passion, and Companionship

Magic not only influences desired outcomes but is also empowering
and fosters personal growth. This process is greatly abetted by the
carefully crafted, tried and tested love spells and rites of romance in
this chapter. Covering every aspect of amour, you can learn spells that
create the potential for love, draw the attention and devotion of a
suitor, strengthen the union between an existing couple, invoke
passion, and, perhaps most importantly, fill your own heart with love
and compassion. Why spend a Saturday evening alone when you
already know the object of your desire? And why doubt your power to
attract love when a little herbal chemistry can make you virtually
irresistible? Your affections will be returned threefold with the treasury
of charms in this compendium.

Attract, Create, and Keep Love in Your Life

Like many before me, love spells were my first. At the age of 14, I cast my first, and soon my best friend was the object of amorous attention from a previously disinterested suitor. Since then, I have had many years and ample opportunity to perfect this most joyous aspect of the craft. I have happily watched these spells kindle and keep love's passion alive time and again.

Any metaphysician will tell you the most common requests for help involve matters of the heart. Witchcraft is based in the knowledge that our destinies lie in our own hands, even where love is concerned. Why suffer the slings and arrows of romance gone wrong when you can do something about it? Here are lots of ideas for magical workings so you have a life you love and a life filled with love.

Light of Love: Altar Dedication

Bring love into your life with this altar dedication. Use a small table or chest in your bedroom and cover it with a rich, red scarf or cloth. Adorn it with objects that signify love—red candles, ruby-colored bowls, roses, a statue of Adonis, a heart-shaped chunk of amethyst, whatever stirs your feelings and senses. Give the area a good smudging to purify the space to refresh it for new beginnings. Anoint your candles with oil of jasmine, rose, or any scent that is redolent of romance to you and prepare some similar incense. Light both and speak aloud:

I light the flame,
I fan the flame.
Each candle I burn is a wish,
I desire and will be desired in return.

Twin-Hearts Candle Consecration

If you are seeking a soul mate, this simple spell will do the trick. At nearly any new-age bookshop, you can find heart-shaped, semiprecious stones. On the next new moon, take two pieces of rose quartz and stand in the center of your bedroom. Light two pink candles and recite the words on the right.

Keep the candles and crystals on your bedside table and think of it as shrine to love. Repeat three nights in a row and ready yourself for amour.

Beautiful crystal I hold this night,
Flame with love for my delight.
Harm to none as love comes to me.
This I ask and so shall it be.

Mists of Avalon Potion

3 drops rose oil

3 drops lavender oil

3 drops neroli (orange blossom) essence

½ cup (120ml) pure distilled water

If you are dreaming of real romance, you can bring about visions of your future true love with this potent potion.

Pour all the ingredients into a colored-glass spray bottle and shake well three times. Fifteen minutes before you retire, spray lightly on your linens, towel, and pillowcase. Keep a dream journal on your nightstand so you can record details of the great love that will soon manifest.

First Moon of New Love: Candle Bell Spell

If you are in a phase of your life where you wish to attract new love, try this Candle Bell Spell two days before the full moon.

1 pink votive candle
A tray
1 long-stemmed red rose bud
A small hand bell
Rose essential oil

Check your lunar almanac and on the first night of the full moon, place the candle on the tray on your altar. Lay the rose bud and bell beside the candle. Anoint the candle with the rose essential oil. For the next two nights, cup the candle in your hands and direct loving thoughts into its flame for at least 5 minutes. On the last night of the full moon, take a thorn from the rose and carve the name of your heart's desire into the candle wax, reciting:

I will find true love.
Light the candle and ring the bell thrice, saying:
As this candle begins to burn, a lover true will I earn.
As this flame burns ever higher, I will feel my lover's fire.

Ring the bell three more times and allow the candle to burn for a few minutes while gazing at the flame. Keep notes in your bedside journal or your Book of Shadows and note how long it takes for true love to walk into your life. It will be interesting to look back and see where it happens, what sign the moon and sun are in, and all the details that will inform your future magical workings.

Dreaming Devotion

This charm will help you see whether a newfound interest will become long term. If you lack clarity on this issue, your dreams can guide you. Use this talisman for clairvoyance.

A small red pouch

1 teaspoon each of dried lavender, dried thyme, and cloves

Bolline

1 vanilla bean pod

12 inches (30cm) red string or cord

Take the small red pouch and place the lavender, thyme, and cloves into it. Using your bolline, cut the vanilla bean pod into two pieces and place them in the bag. Now cut the red string or cord in two, using your sacred knife. Close the bag by tying it with the two sections of cord and hold the pouch in both hands until your warmth and energy fully infuse the potpourri inside. Recite:

Venus guide my dreams tonight—is he [or she] the one?

I dream of devotion and a lifetime of love.

Please give me your answers from the heavens above.

So mote it be. Blessed be.

Tuck your talisman under your pillow. Upon waking, think of your dream. You will receive your answer immediately.

Wanderful Invocation of Love

All of us want our home to be a welcoming place for love and contentment for ourselves and our significant other. You can greatly abet that outcome with this simple spell for binding love.

2 pink candles

Rose essential oil

2 long-stemmed pink roses

Rose incense and incense burner

2 rose quartz crystals, of any size

A tray to hold all these elements

Your wand for love magic (see opposite)

Place all your ritual elements on the tray. Go to your bedroom and place the tray on your nightstand or another chest or table nearest your bed. Anoint your wand and both candles with the rose essential oil and place the roses and the quartz crystals beside the candles. Now light the candles and incense. Pick up your wand and intone aloud:

This is a place where joy lives.
This is a room where my heart gives.
Here is a temple to love and delight.
Here is a home filled with bliss and light.
Blessed be, and so it is.

With your wand, draw a heart shape twice in the wafting smoke of the incense while saying "I love _____." Stand, eyes closed, while visualizing you and your partner enjoying each other's company, happy and in love. End the ritual by saying: "Blessed be." I recommend keeping the tray in your bedroom where it can be a mini shrine to love.

Timing Is Everything: Love Signs

* If you want to strike up a conversation with the handsome, shy fellow at work, try it when the sun is in Gemini, Libra, or Aquarius, the best times for communication.

* If, after a few successful dates, you are looking for things to heat up, fix an aphrodisiac dinner one Taurus or Scorpio moon evening, the most sensual of times.

* Declaring your true love will go very well during the fiery signs of Aries, Leo, or Sagittarius.

* If you want to rekindle a long-lost love, try it when either the sun or the moon are in the signs of Pisces or Cancer, when sentiments run high. As ever, timing is everything, and certain days are made for love.

* You'll have your best success in romancing an ambitious amour during the earthy signs of Capricorn, Taurus, and Virgo. You will probably find them while you are networking or building an empire.

Love Magic Wands

In the section "The Witch's Toolkit" you learned how to make your own wand (see page 22). Here is what you need to know about the perfect wand to use in rituals for romance:

* Almond is a sweet wood and smoother than many; it is excellent for love magic.

* Beech grants wishes, so be careful what you wish for!

* Birch is a wood that is very powerful for new beginnings.

* Ivy wood is related to women's mysteries and will bind people together.

* Lilac wands create beauty, harmony, and happiness and bring you love.

* Rosewood makes the ultimate wand for spellwork conjuring true, lasting love.

Flower Charm

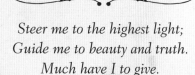

Steer me to the highest light;
Guide me to beauty and truth.
Much have I to give.
Much have I to live.
Bright blessings to one and all.

To light the flower of love in your heart, time this charm with the waning of a new Moon. Place a green candle beside a white lily, rose, or freesia. Make sure it is a posy of personal preference. White flowers have the greatest perfume, and any one of these beauties will impart your home with a pleasing aura. I like to float a gardenia in a clear bowl of fresh water, truly the essence of the divine. Light the candle and hold the flower close to your heart. Pray using the spell on the left.

The Art of Spellbinding: Knotted Heartstrings

On a small piece of paper, write the name of the person whose affection you seek in red ink, then roll into a scroll. Anoint the paper with rose oil. Tie the scroll with red thread, speaking one line of the spell on the right per knot.

Keep the scroll on your love altar and burn red candles anointed with rose oil each evening until your will is done. Be very sure of your heart's desire as this spell is everlasting.

One knot to seek my love,
one to find my love.
One to bring my love, one to bind my love.
Forever bound together as one.
So mote it be; this charm is done.

Candied Herbs

The gift of homemade candy is a marvelous way to signal a crush. One of the byproducts of making herbal honey, liqueurs, and oxymels are the candied herbs, which can also be made especially for snacks and for use in sweet-cakes and cookies.

Stir the liquids together in a big pot and heat slowly, stirring every few minutes. Upon reaching boiling point, add the herbs until well mixed. Turn to a slow simmer until the liquid is very thick and sticky. Spoon the herbs out and place on waxed paper to crystallize. Good herbs for this are hyssop, ginger root, lavender, lemon balm, fennel seed, mint, angelica stems, and thyme, as well as small slivers of orange, lime, and lemon.

1 cup (240ml) vodka

1 cup (240ml) simple sugar syrup (see page 102)

1 cup (240ml) honey

2 cups (50g) dried herb of choice

1 large sheet of waxed paper

✳

SLOW COOKERS—FAST RESULTS

Crock-Pots, or slow cookers, became popular in the early 1970s when many women entered the workplace and this humble, helpful appliance could simmer away the evening's supper throughout the day. Along the way, they also became a staple of many pagans' lives, as they are excellent for mulling cider and wine, melting wax for candles, and all manner of crafts and cookery. They are simply the best for soups, stews, and brews, which greatly benefit from the time when flavors can blend together. For candying herbs and the slow work of decoctions, the slow cooker is a marvelous time saver.

Spell for New Beginnings

This spell can be used to meet someone new or to bring on an exciting new phase in an existing relationship.

1 pink candle and 1 blue candle
Rose or jasmine essential oil
1 or more favorite flowers
A bobby pin/hair grip or safety pin

Before dawn, anoint each candle with rose or jasmine essential oil and place them on your altar. Light both candles, lay the flower(s) next to them, and chant:

Healing starts with new beginnings, please show me who.
My heart is open, I'm ready now.
Today, my heart is open to love anew.
Goddess, you will show me how.
So mote it be.

Extinguish the candles and leave them on your altar. Pin the flower(s) to your lapel, jacket pocket, or in your hair and await the sweet message from the Goddess.

Spice Up Your Life Spell

Start a fresh chapter in your love life without delay with this cup of love.

Cinnamon spice tea (from a shop) or 3 chopped cinnamon sticks
1 cup (240ml) of hot water
1 teaspoon honey
1 teaspoon ground cinnamon (or 3 more sticks ground in your mortar and pestle)

Brew and steep the tea for at least 3 minutes. Stir in the honey and savor the sweet, spicy smell. Drink it while contemplating your hopes, intentions, and dreams for a happy, healthy love life. Now, sprinkle the ground version of this charismatic spice on the threshold of your front door and along your entry path. When the cinnamon powder is crushed underfoot, its regenerative powers will help heat things up in your love life.

Spelling Love

Jasmine and rose have very powerful love vibrations to attract and charm a lover. This simple spell, said aloud, will create loving magic.

1 white candle

Jasmine essential oil

Rose essential oil

Anoint the candle with both essential oils and close your eyes. Say to yourself:

Venus, cast your light on me,
A goddess for today I'll be.
A lover, strong and brave and true,
I seek as a reflection of you.

Now open your eyes and gaze at the candlelight. Venus, goddess of love, has heard you.

Swipe Left for Love: App Enchantment

We all know many people find romance on dating websites and apps. Use your witchy tools of a pendulum (see page 13) and a whispered spell for swift and accurate swiping!

Still the pendant and hold it over the photo on the app of people who may be of interest to you, and then ask it to indicate yes and no. When you get a yes, swipe away! When you have found a person of interest, craft your first message to them, and speak this spell:

God of love, fly my letter hence at the speed of light.
May the arrow of love find a mate so right.
With harm to none and blessing for all.
And so it is.

Now, hit send. Make sure to have a charming response at the ready!

Attracting That Attractive Stranger

Don't tell me you have never had a brief but meaningful encounter at your local café or exchanged long glances on the bus crossing town. Shyness tied your tongue, and now your only hope is that chance will bring you together. Try this trusty attraction spell.

A man-shaped mandrake root or substitute (see spell)

1 cup (20g) of red, white, and pink rose petals

1 red, 1 white, and 1 pink candle

2 goblets of red wine

Place the mandrake root (commonly available at herbalists and metaphysical shops) on your altar. If you cannot find the mandrake root, you could substitute any statue, drawing, photograph, or figure of a man that reflects some quality of your heart's desire. Surround the root or figure's base with the rose petals and candles. Place the goblets with a small amount of red wine in them beside the candles. Make sure it is a wine you really like and would want to share with a romantic interest, as you will refill the goblet each evening. Burn the candles for 5 minutes every night for a week, starting on Friday, Venus's Day.

Sip from one of the goblets, and recite:

Merry Stranger, friend of my heart,
Merry may we meet again.
Hail, fair fellow, friend well met,
I share this wine and toast you,
As we merry meet and merry part
And merry meet again.

Make sure you look your best when you step out as you will soon lock eyes again.

Flirty Friday Date-Night Magic

1 cup (240ml) sesame oil
5 drops orange blossom oil
3 drops rose oil
3 drops amber oil

The touch of Venus makes this the most festive day of the week. This is also the optimal evening for a tryst! To prepare yourself for a romantic and flirtatious Friday night, you must take a goddess bath with the following potion, stored in a special and beautiful bottle or bowl.

Combine the oils and stir with your fingers six times, silently repeating three times:

> *I am a daughter of Venus; I embody love.*
> *My body is a temple of pleasure; I am all that is beautiful.*
> *Tonight, I will drink fully from the cup of love.*

Pour two-thirds of this potion into a steaming bath and meditate upon your evening plans. As you finish, repeat the Venus spell once more.

Don't use a towel but allow your skin to dry naturally. Dress up in your finest goddess garb. Dab a bit of the Venusian oil mix on your pulse points, your wrists, ankles, and the base of your throat. When you are out and about this evening, you will most certainly meet lovely and stimulating new people who are very interested in you. In fact, they are being drawn to you.

Aphrodite's Ageless Skin Potion

You will notice that many a witch appears ageless. There is a good reason for this; we manifest a lot of joy in our life, including creating potions to take excellent care of our skin for Aphrodite-like youthfulness.

Combine these oils in a sealable, dark-blue bottle. Shake very thoroughly and prepare to anoint your skin with this invocation:

¼ cup (60ml) sweet almond oil (as a base)

2 drops chamomile oil

2 drops rosemary oil

2 drops lavender oil

Goddess of Love, Goddess of Light, hear this prayer,
Your youth, beauty, and radiance, please share.
So mote it be.

Clean your skin with warm water, then gently daub with the potion. You can also make a salve or balm using my recipe if you want to turn the clock backward. Prepare to be asked for your beauty secrets.

Anointed Lips

The ripest fruit,
The perfect petal,
Each kiss is a spell
of utmost bliss.
And so it is.

From time immemorial, witches have enchanted with their magical beauty. That is because we know how to supplement Mother Nature's gifts. Before a special evening, employ a "kiss of glamour" by adding one drop of clove oil to your favorite pot of lip gloss. While stirring gently, say the words on the left aloud three times.

This will make your lips tingle in a delightful way and give your kisses a touch of spice. The lucky recipient of your affection will be spellbound.

Belles Lettres: RSVP for Romance

Love letters are a very old art that deepen intimacy. What heart doesn't surge when the object of affection pours passion onto a page? Magic ink, prepared paper, and wax will seal the deal. Take a special sheet of paper—sumptuous handmade paper or creamy watermarked fine stationery is ideal—and write with enchanted ink, such as wine-dark dragonsblood, easily found at any metaphysical shop. Perfume the letter with the signature scent or oil your lover prefers, such as amber, vanilla, or ylang-ylang. Seal the letter with a wax, which you have also scented with one precious drop of this oil and, of course, a kiss.

Before your love letter is delivered, light a candle anointed with this oil of love and intone this spell:

> *Eros, speed my message on wings of desire.*
> *Make my sweetheart burn with love's pure fire.*
> *So mote it be.*

Be ready for an ardent answer!

GROW A GARDEN OF EARTHLY DELIGHTS

A happy relationship can be cultivated, literally. By planting and
carefully tending plants that have special properties—
night-blooming jasmine for heightened sensuality and scent,
lilies for lasting commitment, roses for romance—you can
nurture your marriage or partnership. During a new moon in the
Venus-ruled signs of Taurus or Libra, plant an array of flowers
that will enhance mutual devotion.

Gypsy Love Herbs

Many a gypsy woman has enjoyed the fruits of long-lasting love by reciting the following
charm while mixing rye and pimento into a dish shared with the object of her affection.
While stirring in these amorous herbs, declaim:

> *Rye of earth, pimento of fire,*
> *Eaten surely lights desire.*
> *Serve to he whose love I crave,*
> *And his heart I will enslave!*

Oil of Love

Indulge in this sensually satisfying ritual concoction that will make your skin glow and will also surround you with a seductive aura. Your personal vibration will draw people toward you thanks to this lovely essence.

2 tablespoons (30ml) sweet almond carrier (or base) oil

6 drops jasmine essential oil

6 drops rose essential oil

1 ounce (30g) aloe vera gel

3-ounce (85ml) squeeze bottle

1 tablespoon (15ml) rose water

1 pink candle

1 stick of rose incense

Timing: Perform this ritual on a moonlit night.

Place all the oils, rose water, and the aloe vera gel into your squeeze bottle. Shake the mixture well. As you undress, imagine you are preparing for the one you love. Light the pink candle and rose incense and say:

My heart is open, my spirit soars.
Goddess bring my love to me. Blessed be.

Now, pour the Oil of Love into your palm and gently rub into your skin. As you do so, dream of what delights are heading your way.

Ultimate Glamour

Few people know that the word "glamour" comes from the seventeenth-century Scottish word "glamour," which meant to cast a spell or enchantment over anyone who looks upon you.

During the waxing moon, take the rings, necklace, and earrings you are planning to wear during a special tryst and lay them on your altar to imbue them with magic. Mix together one tablespoon each of the dried herbs vervain, thistle, chamomile, and elderflower. Cover your jewelry with the herb mixture and then sprinkle salt on top. Leave for at least 5 minutes, then shake off the herbs and pick up your gems. Hold the jewelry in your hands and chant:

Bless these jewels and the hand and heart of the wearer with the light of heaven above.
May all who look upon me
See me through the eyes of love.

Now put on the empowered and enchanted jewelry and go off for your special date.

Enchanted Evening Rite

Take the time to prepare yourself for romance and turn your thoughts to love and sensuality.

Petals of 1 red rose

A large glass or ceramic bowl and a wooden spoon

½ cup (90g) of Epsom salts

½ cup (70g) of baking soda

½ cup (120ml) carrier (or base) oil, ideally jojoba or apricot

6 drops each of jasmine, ylang ylang, and neroli essential oil (or 12 drops of one, if you prefer just one scent)

A soothing bath is the perfect prelude to your date. Make the water warm enough to be relaxing, but not so hot that it makes you sleepy. Mix all the ingredients, except for the rose petals, together in the bowl with the wooden spoon and then add the mixture under the running faucet. The Epsom salts will relax tense muscles and the baking soda combined with the carrier oil will soften your skin. These aphrodisiac essential oils are very potent. Lastly, float the rose petals in the water, and bathe by natural light before nightfall. As the mix of warm water, oils, and bath salts smooths your skin, let it also soothe your soul.

Passion Potion Massage Mix

Jasmine, neroli, amber, and just a touch of vanilla essential oils create a romantic and exotic scent that lingers on your skin for hours.

½ cup (120ml) unscented carrier (or base) oil, ideally jojoba

¼ cup (60ml) jasmine essential oil

10 drops amber essential oil

5 drops neroli essential oil

5 drops vanilla essential oil

Dark-colored, sealable bottle with a dropper cap

Mix all the oils together in the tightly capped bottle and keep in a dark cupboard. Passion Potion will last six months. Remember to always shake well before using.

Body Blissing Spell

If you want to share your Passion Potion with another, before you do, bless the mixture with this spell that will imbue any usage with an optimal loving experience:

Light of love, shine on us here
Help us to let go of any doubt and fear
Brighten all hearts with your light so clear.
Bring us all close, those we hold dear.
Light of love, love is near.
So mote it be.

Merry Meet Medieval Brew

You need to start this special mixture by pouring a gallon (3.8 liters) of unfiltered sweet apple cider into a cauldron. You can buy the cider but it is even better if you make it from apples you have gathered or harvested. Take a bottle of your favorite low-cost red wine and heat gently in the pot on a low flame; add sugar, cinnamon, and cloves to your taste, but at least a tablespoon of each. Pour the cider into the warmed wine and add 13 whole cloves and 6 cinnamon sticks, then stir widdershins (counterclockwise) every six minutes. Notice how your entire home fills with the spicy sweetness of merriment. After 30 minutes, your brew should be ready to serve.

Cinnamon Liqueur

✳

DIY ELIXIR

You can make a simple syrup, a base for any liqueur, in five short minutes by boiling 1 cup (200g) of sugar in ½ cup (120ml) of water.

You can create distinctive after-dinner drinks and digestives by adding whole herbs into simple syrup and letting them steep: try using angelica, anise, bergamot, hyssop, all mints, fennel, and, maybe the most special of all, violets. To your health!

1 cup (240ml) vodka

2 cloves

1 teaspoon ground coriander seed

1 cinnamon stick

1 cup (240ml) simple sugar syrup (see left)

This popular pagan beverage gives peppy energy and can also be a love potion. These few ingredients can lead to a lifetime of devotion.

Pour the vodka into a bowl and add the herbs. Cover with a clean, dry towel and place in a cupboard for two weeks. Strain and filter until the result is a clear liquid into which you add the simple syrup and place back on the shelf for a week. Store this in a pink- or red-capped bottle; you now have liquid love. You can add this to hot chocolate, water, tea, or milk for a delightful drink to share with a partner.

Passion Potion Spell

Lower the lamps, light red candles, and enjoy a warm cup of cocoa with a shot of the cinnamon liqueur. Speak this spell aloud as you are preparing the libation—you will radiate passion and draw your lover to you with this enchantment:

> *Today, I awaken the goddess in me.*
> *By surrendering to my love for thee.*
> *Tonight, I will heat the night with my fire.*
> *As we drink this cup, we awaken desire.*
> *I am alive! I am love. So mote it be.*

"I love how all-encompassing the creation of magic potions can be: you start with a handful of seeds, tend your herb garden, and end up with a pantry filled with libations that are at once medicinal, delicious, celebratory, and, most importantly, crafted with loving care."

Seal It with a Kiss: Binding Love Potion

When we are in love, we all hope for it to be requited. Spellcraft can help with that! Here's one to share with your lover.

2 teaspoons dried lemon balm, basil, blackberry, or magnolia buds

2 cups (480ml) of water

A teapot

2 mugs

Honey, to sweeten

To ensure a faithful relationship, make a tea from any of these herbs of loyalty in love. Boil the water and add to the teapot along with the herbs. Steep for 3 minutes, then pour the tea into the mugs and sweeten with honey. Intone this spell as you stir each cup.

Lover be faithful, lover be true.
This is all I am asking of you.
Give thy heart to nobody but me.
This is my will.
So mote it be.

Before you and your lover share this special treat together, whisper this wish in secret:

Honey magnolia [or whichever herb you chose], Goddess's herb,
Perform for me enchantment superb,
Let _____ [name of lover] and I be as one.
As ever, harm to none.

With this, the spell is done.

This spell must be sealed with a kiss between you and your beloved. Now enjoy drinking the tea with the object of your affection, from whom you wish not to stray, and his or her loyalty will never sway.

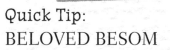

Quick Tip:
BELOVED BESOM

If you and your spouse were joined in marriage with a traditional "old school" Wiccan handfasting, wherein you jumped over the broom, known as a besom, hang it in your bedroom near your bed. These besoms are often beribboned so use another ribbon as the hanger as you should not use a nail. This broom will serve as a happy reminder of your vows of love to each other.

Brewing Up a Batch of Passion

For a passionate pick-me-up, drink this tasty tonic with your lover.

½ cup (120ml) of lemonade

2 mugs

2 cups (480ml) of water

½ cup (50g) of sliced fresh ginger root

1 teaspoon cardamom

Honey, to sweeten

Pour half of the lemonade into each mug. Boil the ginger and cardamom in the water for 4 minutes, strain, then pour into the mugs and sweeten with honey to taste. Before you drink this lustful libation, simply say:

Gift of the Goddess and magic of moon,
May the flower of our love come to full bloom.

Shared between two lovers before a tryst, this enchanted potion will give great endurance for a memorable encounter. Each sip is full of love's sure power.

Chilled Cucumber Mint Soup for Lovers

3 large, peeled cucumbers
½ cup (15g) fresh mint leaves
1 teaspoon kosher salt
3 tablespoons olive oil

Cucumber has aphrodisiac qualities, according to recent studies, thanks to the veggie's scent. This easy-to-grow delight provides several nutrients essential to maintaining sexual health, including manganese and Vitamins C and K, and it makes for vibrant skin. This is a short and sweet recipe for a refreshingly cold soup to share with a loved one on a hot day.

Put the ingredients in the blender and purée. This gorgeous, green potage makes enough for two servings for a hungry couple. The only accompaniments you need are crispy herb crackers, an icy beverage, and each other.

Be My Valentine: Food Magic

Cucumber is not the only way to set the mood for a night of love. Surprise the object of your affection with one of these treats:

* **Chocolate** is rightly called the "food of the gods."

* **Nutmeg** is held in high regard as an aphrodisiac by Chinese women.

* **Honey**—ever wonder why the time after a wedding is the honeymoon? Bee-sweetened drinks are a must!

* **Oysters** have been celebrated since Roman times for their special aphrodisiac properties.

* **Strawberries** lend a very sweet erotic taste—serve together with chocolate for maximum effect.

* **Vanilla** is little known for its amorous properties, but the taste and scent are powerful.

Sweetheart Shortbread

⅓ cup (10g) candied herbs (see page 89)

⅓ cup (110g) honey

2 sticks (225g) butter, softened

2½ cups (340g) all-purpose (plain) flour

This shortbread makes an excellent gift for a loved one. Cream the herbs and honey into the softened butter and fold the flour into it gradually. Mix well and roll into a 2-inch-wide (5cm) log shape. Wrap this dough in wax paper and chill in the refrigerator for at least 2 hours. Preheat the oven to 325°F/160°C/gas mark 3. Slice the dough into 6 rounds and place onto a greased cookie sheet. Bake for 20 minutes or until the top is beginning to turn golden.

Lavender and hyssop make the sweetest dessert shortbreads. Alternatively, omit the honey from the recipe and use sage and thyme for a highly satisfying and savory breakfast shortbread to serve your sweetheart after an exquisite evening.

Aphrodisiac Icing

2 tablespoons water

4 drops vanilla extract

6 lemon balm leaves, plus extra for decorating

2 scant cups (270g) confectioner's (icing) sugar

1 lemon

Candied lemon (using recipe on page 89 for candied herbs)

You can mend broken hearts and enchant any would-be love interest with lemon balm. This recipe takes the cake, either one of your own making or a store-bought spongecake. Glaze the Sweetheart Shortbread above with this icing and you will turn anyone who tastes it into your devotee.

Combine the water, vanilla, and lemon balm and soak overnight. Strain out the herbs and add sugar into the liquid. Grate in zest of the lemon and whisk, squeezing in some lemon juice if needed for liquid consistency. Pour this icing over the cake and top with candied lemon and balm. This distinctive dessert is a spell spun of sugar.

Crushing on Coffee

6 cardamom pods

1 cinnamon stick

½ cup (110g) ground coffee beans

6 cups (1.5 liters) water

Cream or another type of creamer (e.g. Half & Half)

1 tablespoon honey or raw sugar

Cardamom is a spice the Indians, creators of the Kama Sutra, used to good effect. Called the "grains of paradise," you can find it in any grocery and recognize the organic kind by the green color of the pods.

Crush the cardamom pods with a pestle and mortar and extract the seeds, discarding the pods. Break the cinnamon into pieces and grind together with the cardamom seeds and stir into the ground coffee. Make coffee as you usually would, using a French press or coffee maker for four cups brimming with bliss. The strong, rich flavor does call for cream and sweetening, so you quite literally sweeten the pot and serve it up for an amorous and energetic evening.

✳

THE BUZZ ON HONEY

We have all had jars of honey crystallize in the cupboard—but think twice before you toss it out; this is the best kind for cooking and improves texture for baked goods.

Lover's Tea

Here is a quick recipe to create exactly the right mood for the dreamiest of evenings.

Stir all the ingredients together in a clockwise motion. You can store this in a tin or colored jar for up to a year for those special occasions. When you are ready to brew the tea, pour boiling water over the herbs, two teaspoons for a cup of water. Say the following spell aloud during the 5-minute steeping and picture your heart's desire.

1 ounce (28g) dried hibiscus flowers

1 ounce (28g) dried and pulverized rosehips

½ ounce (14g) peppermint

½ ounce (14g) dried lemon balm

> *Herbal brew of love's emotion*
> *With my wish I fortify*
> *When two people share this potion*
> *This love shall intensify*
> *As in the Olde Garden of Love.*

Sweeten to taste with honey and share this luscious libation with the one you love.

"At the end of life, all that matters is how much love you gave to the world and how much of your heart you shared with people."

Making Relationships Sacred: Loved-one Shrine

This sacred space is dedicated to the special people in your life: friends, family, and your partner. Your shrine can be a low table or even a shelf and provides a place to put gifts you have received from your loved ones, which might include crystals, jewelry, art, and lovely objects along with all their photos in frames. Every time I see my own special Loved-one Shrine, I smile. It fills my heart with love.

Sage for smudging

A pink cloth or scarf

2 pink candles and 2 white candles

A small rose quartz and fluorite crystals

A vase of fresh cut flowers of your choice (daisies, for example)

To set up your shrine, purify the space by lighting the sage bundle and letting the smoke waft around the area. This is called "smudging" and is an essential part of witchcraft. You can use wild sage or purchase it in any herb store. Once you have smudged the space, cover your sacred space with the scarf or cloth, and place the candles in each of the four corners. (Pink is the color of affection and white represents purity.) Place the crystals around the vase of fresh flowers—whichever ones connote fun and friendship to you. Then add gifts or other trinkets that remind you of your loved one.

Light the candles, kneel before your newly created shine and say:

I light the fire of loyalty
The heat of heart and the flame of love
and friendship.
Brightest blessing, Great Goddess bring,
The spirit of friendship will surely sing.
As the fates do dance, I welcome the chance
To share my love and my life.
So mote it be.

The Flame of Friendship

You can further charge the candles on your Loved-one Shrine by scratching your desire into the wax. I use the thorn of a rose for this and write the words of my intention. Many witches use symbols: a moon, the sun, a flower, a heart, a dollar sign, or a number, for example. You can also inscribe a name.

Take a large solar-hued yellow pillar candle anointed with lemon or bergamot essential oil and charge it with positivity toward your loved ones. Scratch your own name into it and write "I love _____" with the name of your friend or family member.

Light the candle and say four times:

I love me. I love _____.

For a daily dose of one-minute magic, light the candle every night and repeat this love charge before bed and every morning when you arise. Your heart will lift and soar, which then emanates outward toward this special person in your life.

CHAPTER 5

SACRED SELF-CARE

Wellness and Self-discovery

The fast pace of today can cause enormous strain and anxiety. Not only
does this pressure and stress disrupt the joy of every day, but it also
affects your health. The "way of the witch" never lets worry get in the
way of wellness, and these soothing spells will add greatly to your
quality of life. Discover, too, how to explore yourself through ritual.
Creating and performing rites and spells on your own will help you
define and strengthen your sense of identity and customize your
desired outcome according to your individual will and intention.
Carrying out solo rituals means you are in control, a seeker progressing
along the spiritual path at your own speed. Use the spells herein as
examination of your deepest inner self.

Simple Salt Magic

The one thing every household has in the kitchen is salt, either plain white grains or the larger, kosher crystals. This most common of cupboard condiments is also an essential in magic, dating back thousands of years and used by Egyptians, Chaldeans, Babylonians, and early European tribes for purification, protection, and cleansing. Salt is often utilized in hoodoo, sprinkled on doorsteps and pathways to keep bad spirits away (as well as bad people), and added into witch bottles to clear energy. During the era of the early Roman Empire, soldiers were paid in salt—it was that valuable. Long have these grains been used to preserve and improve the taste of foods.

Perhaps the highest purpose of salt is as a healer; it is essential in the diet for good health and external uses in baths and rubs can be enormously relaxing. Salt removes negative energy and can vanquish a headache in short order with the following magical application.

Headache Healer: Salt Serenity Spell

Fill a tea kettle and set it to boil. Pour hot water into a mug and add a full tablespoon of salt. Once it has cooled to a warm temperature, hold the mug against each of your temples in turn and keep it there for a long moment. Dip your forefinger of your left hand into the salt water and gently rub each of your temples and your forehead in circular movements. Sit or lay flat in silence for some time with your eyes closed. If this turns into a nap, all the better.

When you are ready, rise and your headache will be at bay. Place the cup on your kitchen altar for a period of 24 hours so it can draw out any negative energy from your home. The following day, throw the salt water from the cup onto your front step or sidewalk to keep any bad juju away. As you walk down your front path, you'll notice that you feel clear-headed and peaceful.

Setting Sun Spell

The jar of bay leaf in your spice cupboard will get you one step closer to tranquility. To clear energy and prepare for a week of calm clarity, find your favorite white flower—iris, lily, rose, one that is truly beautiful to your eye. Monday's setting sun is the time for this spell, immediately after the sun goes below the horizon. Anoint a white candle with jasmine oil and place on your altar. Take your single white blossom and add that to your altar in a bowl of freshly drawn water. Place a whole bay leaf on a glass dish in front of the lit candle and speak aloud the words of the spell on the right.

Burn the bay leaf in the fire of the candle and put it in the glass dish where it can turn into ash, smudging as it burns.

This fire is pure; this flower is holy;
this water is clear.
These elements purify me.
I walk in light with nothing in my way.
My energy is pure, my spirit is holy,
my being is clear.
Blessed be.

Recharging Weekend Wonder

This natural remedy is an excellent way to refresh after a hectic week.

2 drops rosemary essential oil

3 drops bergamot essential oil

2 drops jasmine essential oil

3 drops lavender essential oil

6 drops carrier oil

A small ceramic or glass bowl

Timing: This tincture is most potent right after the sun sets, by the light of the waxing or full moon.

Blend the essential oils and carrier oil in the bowl. Take off your shoes so you can be more grounded. Walk outside, stand on your deck or by an open window. Now, close your eyes, lift your head to the moon, and recite aloud:

Bright moon goddess, eternal and wise,
Give your strength to me now.
As I breathe, you are alive in me for this night.
Health to all, calm to me.
So mote it be.

Gently rub one drop of this natural remedy potion on each pulse point: both wrists, behind your ear lobes, on the base of your neck, and behind your knees. As the oil surrounds you with its warm scent, you will be filled with a quiet strength.

Lunar Elixir: Restorative Full Moon Infusion

The full moon is a truly auspicious time and one to savor and make the most of. Try this restorative Lunar Elixir anytime your energy level is low to bolster mind, body, and spirit.

1 teaspoon sliced fresh ginger root

1 teaspoon jasmine tea leaves

1 teaspoon peppermint tea leaves

2 cups (480ml) fresh water

A teapot and a mug

Timing: Full moon phases last two days, so make this elixir on the first night at midnight.

Just before midnight, brew and strain an infusion of these healthful and energizing herbs. Once it is cool, pour it into your favorite mug and relish the aromatic steam for a moment. Wait for the stroke of midnight. Now, step outside and drink the elixir during this enchanted hour in the glow of moonlight. You will immediately feel clearer, more centered, and more focused.

Don't Worry, Be Happy: A Spell to Quell Anxiety

As the sun sets on a waning moon day, you can quiet the inner voices of worrywart that get in the way of life. When our moon ebbs, another grows forth, and so it goes for our creativity and renewal cycles.

1 vanilla bean pod

Sandalwood incense

Amber resin

A charcoal cake for burning incense

A fireproof glass or clay dish

1 black or gray candle

Timing: As the moon decreases in size, cast this spell.

Quick Tip: MOON SPELL SECRETS

In late spring and early summer, you will see a shape resembling a dragon on the moon—an auspicious time for new beginnings, business, and magic related to work and money. The moon dragon is visible when Jupiter occupies the center of the sky. Ventures begun under its influence will meet with great success.

Set aside a small piece of the vanilla bean, then grind together a teaspoon each of sandalwood, amber, and the remainder of the vanilla bean using either the back of a spoon or your mortar and pestle. Burn this resin-based mixture on a piece of charcoal in the fireproof dish on your altar. Light the black or gray candle, for protection. Rub the reserved small piece of vanilla bean in your palm until the scent begins to waft up thanks to the heat in your hands. Concentrate on the flame and rub the same vanilla essence on your temples and place your hand over your heart.

As you meditate, think about how you sometimes doubt yourself, worry needlessly, and how you will begin to trust your innate wisdom and instincts. Visualize clearing all anxiety from your mind. Think about the wonderful aspects in your life, your bright future, and your potential as you chant:

La lune, goddess of the moon,
As you may grow, so do I.
Here, tonight, under your darkest light,
I embrace all within me that is good and right,
and bid goodbye to all the rest. Blessed be.

Blow out the candle and throw it into a fireplace or your cast iron cauldron to burn away. You must completely destroy the candle because it contains the energy of your anxiety and fear. Now, go and worry no more.

Waning Moon Contentment Ritual

You can create a week of blissful and composed calm with the following spell.

A purple candle

Hibiscus or violet essential oil

A bouquet of purple flowers
(violets, for example)

Timing: On a Monday, as the moon grows smaller in the sky, try this spell.

On a waning moon Monday evening, anoint your purple candle with the essential oil. Place the candle on your altar beside a vase of fresh violets or other purple flowers. Sit in front of your altar as twilight begins, and when the sun is completely gone, light the candle and chant:

Any care and despair begone.
Here with the mountain, the river, the tree, the grass
and the moon.
I receive my strength from Nature and she is my center.
Tomorrow and the next, all gladness will enter.
Harm to none, only good.

Sanctuary Spell: Rose-water Rite

Three simple ingredients—a pink candle, a red rose, and water—can bestow a powerful steadying and calming influence. The rose signifies beauty, love for yourself and others, blossoming, budding, the earth, your heart, and peace. The candle stands for the yellow flame of the East, unity, harmony, focus, higher intention, and the light of the soul. Water is cleansing, free flowing, affects emotions, and stands for the West. This spell can be done alone or in a group where you pass the bowl around.

Timing: Sun or moon in Venus-ruled Libra is a sweet time to share this rite with those you care for.

Float a red rose in a clear bowl of water, and light a pink candle beside the rose. With the fingers of your left hand, gently stir the water and speak aloud this blessing:

I give myself life and health, refreshing water for my spirit.
I give myself time to rest, and space to grow.
I am love. My heart is as big as the world.
I am peace of mind. So be it, now and always.

Awaken the Imagination: Age of Aquarius Spell

Often, our state of mind grows restless when life becomes too routine. Inspiration and imagination will remedy this instantly.

1 green candle
1 yellow candle
An amethyst crystal
A green apple
A small pine branch

Timing: Check your favorite celestial calendar to plan this spell for when the moon is in the sign of brilliance, Aquarius.

At one hour before midnight, place the two candles on your altar. Next to them, place the crystal, apple, and pine branch.

At 11:11 pm, hold the apple in the palm of your right hand and speak the following spell while circling the candlelit altar clockwise four times:

Sun and moon, awaken me tonight
With the power of Earth and Air, Fire and Water.
As I bite this fruit of knowledge, I am inspired.
All possibilities are before me. And so it is.

Eat the apple, then bury the seeds in your garden or in a potted plant. You will walk on a path new with promise of anything you can imagine. Keep the crystal and pine on your altar for as long as you wish and they will spark inspiration every time you see them.

Bay Leaf Balm

Any body oil or herbal oil can be turned into a salve with the addition of wax. The ratio for a body salve is 3 ounces (90ml) coconut oil to 1 ounce (30ml) beeswax. Use a double boiler to heat the oil and wax until completely melted. Test the viscosity of your salve by pouring a dab onto a cold plate. If satisfied with the consistency, pour off into clean jars to cool. If you need to add more wax, now is the time to do it.

Balms are simply salves with the addition of essential oils. Add two drops of eucalyptus essential oil and two drops of lemon oil while the mix is still warm. Now add the bay leaf: if you have a bay laurel tree, pick some fresh leaves, or you can also go to your spice rack and take three leaves from the jar and grind them in your mortar and pestle until broken up into fine, little pieces. Sprinkle the finely crushed bay laurel into the oil and wax, stir well, and seal to preserve the aroma.

Bay leaf balm will have a wonderfully calming effect anytime you use it and can be rubbed on your temples when you need to de-stress. I recommend Sunday night soaks, where you slather on the balm before stepping into a hot bath. Take a washcloth and massage your skin, then lie back and relax for 20 minutes. When you drain the bathtub, your stress will also empty out, and you can start your week afresh, ready to handle anything that comes your way.

Body Purification Ritual Bath

Since the time of the ancients in the Mediterranean and Mesopotamia, salts of the sea combined with soothing oils have been used to purify the body by way of gentle, ritualized rubs. From Bathsheba to Cleopatra, these natural salts have been used to smooth the skin and enhance circulation, which is vital to overall physical health as skin is the single largest organ in the human body. Dead Sea salts have long been a popular export and are readily available at most health food shops and spas. You can make your own salts, however, and not only control the quality and customize the scent, but save money, too. The definitive benefit that is far above the cost savings is that you can imbue your concoction with your intention, which is absolutely imperative when you are performing rites of self-healing,

Shekinah's Garden of Eden Salts

Shekinah translates to "She who dwells within" and is the Hebrew name for the female aspect of God. Olden legend has it that she co-created the world side by side with Yahweh, the god of Israel. This simple recipe recalls the scents and primal memories of that edenic paradise.

3 cups (385g) Epsom salts

½ cup (120ml) sweet almond oil

1 tablespoon glycerin

4 drops ylang-ylang essential oil

2 drops jasmine essential oil

Mix well and store in a colored and well-capped glass bottle. Prepare for the ritual rub by lighting citrus- and rose-scented candles. Step out of your clothes and hold the salts in the palms of your hand. Pray aloud:

> *Shekinah, may your wisdom guide me,*
> *My body is a temple to you.*
> *Here I worship today, with heart*
> *and hands,*
> *Body and soul.*
> *I call upon you for healing,*
> *Shekinah, bring me breath and life.*
> *Ancient one, I thank you*
> *With heart and hands,*
> *Body and soul.*

Use these salts with a clean washcloth or new sponge and gently scrub your body while standing in the shower or bathtub. The ideal time is during a waxing morning moon or at midnight during a new moon. You will glow with health and inner peace.

Sensual Soak: Scorpio Moon Rite

Moon in Scorpio is the time to explore bodily pleasures. Sandalwood, amber, and vetiver are all rich, earthy scents that combine well together.

5 drops sandalwood essential oil

5 drops amber essential oil

2 drops vetiver essential oil

½ cup (90g) Epsom salts

½ cup (70g) baking soda

Combine the essential oils with the Epsom salts and stir in the baking soda. Mix well to create a richly scented paste. You can use a couple of different ways: either slather it onto yourself and shower off with a loofah and thick washcloth or, and this is my favorite way to soak up this earthly pleasure, roll it into a ball after you mix it and place under the faucet as you are running a hot bath. The entire room will smell like paradise. Soak it all in, lie back, and enjoy this fully.

If you want to keep this for the future or give as a thoughtful gift, you can store in a lidded container or roll into bath bombs and let them dry on wax paper or paper towels. This recipe can make three palm-size bath bombs.

Venus Rising Invocation

Coconut milk creates a rich, moisturizing bath and leaves skin silky smooth. Ylang ylang is a heady, exotic scent that is lightened and heightened by the citrusy note of the orange.

2 drops ylang ylang essential oil

3 drops orange essential oil

1 can (14fl oz/400ml) of coconut milk

Timing: Both Venus-ruled Taurus and Libra sun and moon signs are very romantic, making them the perfect times for this goddess invocation.

Combine the essential oils with the coconut milk and add to a tubful of warm water.

Pray aloud to Venus:

Goddess of love and grace,
Bringer of all we so enjoy.
Fill both me and this space
With felicity, peace, and joy.
With harm to none, so mote it be.

Calm Emotion Potion

Why does every day seem like it is as long as a week nowadays? Unplugging from cable news and constant social media feeds will help, as will this time-tested aromatherapy healing potion. This remedy is an excellent way to recharge and refresh after a very hectic week.

A small ceramic or glass bowl

2 drops bergamot essential oil

2 drops vanilla essential oil

1 drop amber essential oil

2 drops lavender essential oil

4 drops carrier (or base) oil, apricot or sesame, ideally

Timing: This tincture is most potent right after the sun sets, by the light of the moon.

Mix all the oils together in the bowl.

Take off your shoes so you can be more grounded. Walk outside, and stand on your veranda or by an open window. Now, close your eyes, lift your head to the moon, and recite aloud:

Bright moon goddess, eternal and wise, give your strength to me now.
As I breathe, you are alive in me for this night.
Health to all, calm to me.
So mote it be.

Gently rub one drop of Calm Emotion Potion on each pulse point: on both wrists, behind your ear lobes, on the base of your neck, and behind your knees. Close your eyes and breathe the sweetly serene scent in as you stand barefoot for 5 full minutes. If you need more time to restore yourself and regain your calm, continue your mindful breathing and contemplation. As the oil surrounds you with its warm scent, you will be filled with a quiet strength.

Waters of Wellness

For thousands of years, we humans have been "taking the waters" as a way to restore, and also heal illness. A ritual bath that will simultaneously relax and stimulate you, is a rare and wonderful thing.

4 cups (720g) of Epsom salts

A large glass bowl

½ cup (120ml) of almond carrier (or base) oil

6 drops comfrey essential oil

4 drops eucalyptus essential oil

4 drops rosemary essential oil

6 drops bergamot essential oil

Pour the salts into the bowl and fold in the carrier (or base) oil. Now add in the essential oils, stirring after each is added. Continue to blend the mixture until it is moistened thoroughly. You can add more almond oil if necessary.

When your bath tub is one-quarter full, add one-quarter of the salt mixture under the faucet. Breathe in deeply ten times, inhaling and exhaling fully before you recite this:

Healing spirits I offer myself to you.
Remove from me any impurities
Of the spirit and mind, I open myself to you,
Body, heart, and soul.
With harm to none and healing to me, so mote it be.

When the tub is full, step inside and exercise your breath ten more times. Repeat the prayer while you use the rest of the salts to scrub your body, carefully avoiding your eye area. Rest and rejuvenate as long as you like while visualizing your renewed health and vigor.

Weekend Me-time: Relaxation Massage Oil Blend

Weekends are the best time for taking good care of yourself. We all need to practice self-care more than ever now that the world seems so chaotic and life is crazy-busy. Sandalwood, lavender, and clary sage create a deeply soothing blend with a sensuous scent. It is both restful and stimulating—the perfect combination.

6 drops sandalwood essential oil

6 drops lavender essential oil

6 drops clary sage essential oil

½ cup (120ml) jojoba or almond carrier (or base) oil

Dark-colored, sealable bottle with a dropper cap

1 cup (240ml) warm water

Put the essential oils and carrier oil into the dark-colored, sealable bottle. Carefully cap the bottle and gently shake until the oils have blended together. Store the bottle in a dark cupboard. Before using it on yourself or a loved one, shake well. You can warm it by putting the sealed bottle in a cup of warm water and let it sit there for 4 minutes. Many masseuses pour the oil into their palm and let their own body heat warm it. Either way adds to the relaxation factor.

Saturday Spell for Contacting Spirits

Outside the witchy world, it is not well known that Saturday is the optimal day for contacting those who have passed from this realm to the next. When Samhain, to mark the end of the harvest season, falls on a Saturday, it gives a big boost to our ability to make contact through the veil between the worlds. After nightfall, you can speak to lost loved ones or others with whom you desire contact.

An amethyst of the deepest, darkest purple, obsidian, and/or rainbow moonstone (see spell)

Your Book of Shadows and a pen

Strong-smelling incense, such as frankincense, nag champa, or sandalwood

A fireproof clay or glass dish

Sage for smudging

You can either use one of each of the three crystals, or three of the same kind of crystal. Sit in a comfortable position on the floor or on a pillow with your Book of Shadows and pen nearby. I learned from High Priestess Z. Budapest that "the dead love incense; the stronger the better and it will call them to you." Light the incense in the fireproof dish and pass the crystals through the smoke. Then touch your third eye with one of the crystals for a moment and picture the person you want to contact. Place that crystal by the dish of sweet-smelling smoky incense. Take the other two crystals in your hand and speak this spell aloud:

Great Goddess, I call ___ [speak the name of the spirit] forth now.
From this side, to you, will I bow.
Words of wisdom, we need here and now.
Peace and love is here, I vow.
With harm to none, Blessed be thou.

Now pass your Book of Shadows through the incense smoke and start writing down the messages. Whatever comes into your mind is what you are meant to know. After a few moments, thank the spirit and say goodbye, directing it back to its side of the veil. Extinguish the incense and light the sage and give a very good smudging to the area. Place your Book of Shadows on your altar and consider the message this generous spirit has given you.

Saffron Serenity Spell

This evening ritual is a wonderful way to end the day. Light a yellow candle for mental clarity, and anoint it with calming and uplifting bergamot oil. Place a yellow rose in a vase to the left of the candle. To the right, place a bowl containing at least two citrine or quartz crystals.

Saffron water is made by boiling a single teaspoon of saffron from your cupboard in 2 quarts (2 liters) of distilled water. Let cool to room temperature and pour into the bowl of crystals. Put your hands together as in prayer and dip your hands in the bowl. Touch your third eye in the center of your forehead, anointing yourself with the saffron water. Now, speak aloud:

Goddess great, fill me with your presence
This night, I am whole and at peace.
Breathing in, breathing out,
I feel your safe embrace.
And so it is.

The Serenity Spectrum

I have already explained how powerful candles can be (see page 16), but did you know you can burn colored candles on certain days of the week for all kinds of well-being? The guide below shows which candles to use and when.

* For inner peace, burn silver candles on Monday.

* To let go of anger, burn orange candles on Tuesday.

* For mental clarity, burn yellow candles on Wednesday.

* For a peaceful home, burn blue candles on Thursday.

* For kindness and compassion, burn pink candles on Friday.

* For success at work and for physical well-being, burn green candles on Friday.

* To overcome regret or guilt, burn white candles on Saturday.

* For self-confidence and to overcome fear, burn red candles on Sunday.

"Every day, you can renew your own health and wellness in many small ways; a cup of green tea with a morning prayer can be a simple rite that gives you calm and greater wellness."

Invoke Your Inner Goddess: Divine Essence Oil

This relaxation remedy is an excellent way to create personal space after a hectic week.

2 drops cedar essential oil

2 drops sandalwood essential oil

2 drops amber essential oil

2 drops lavender essential oil

4 drops carrier (or base) oil, such as sesame or jojoba

A small bowl or vial, preferably heart-hued red

Timing: This tincture is most potent on goddess Freya's Day, Friday evening.

Mix together the essential oils with the carrier (or base) oil in the bowl or vial.

Touch one drop of the Divine Essence Oil on each pulse point: on both wrists, behind your ear lobes, on the base of your neck, and behind your knees. Wait a few moments and let the power of the goddess fill your senses as your mind, body, and spirit are renewed. Close your eyes and recite:

Freya, eternal and wise, give your strength to me now.
As I breathe, you are alive in me for this night.

Make sure to thank the goddess for all the blessings in your life.

Conjuring Cords

For ridding yourself of something (or someone) undesirable, try this spell.

Timing: Ideally this should be done during the waning moon.

Take 3 feet of string or fabric cord in banishing colors of gray or black. Begin tying knots as you chant:

By knot of one, my charms begun,
By two, my charms come true,
By knot of three, my desire is free.
By four, I shall have more.
By knot of five, I will thrive,
By six, ill fortune I nix.
By knot of seven, to Jove in heaven.
So mote it be.

Once you have finished, the string or cord should be given back to the earth by burying it in the ground or tossing it into a body of water, preferably a river.

Spell for Letting Go

Most of us have had problems giving up on a relationship at one time or another.

A piece of black string, enough to tie around your waist

Bolline

A photo or memento representing your ex

Timing: Ideally this should be done during the waning moon when things can be put to rest, but it works anytime you need it. Listen to your heart and you'll know exactly when it is required.

Tie the black string around your waist during the waning moon. Tie something symbolic from the old relationship to the end of the string —a photo or the name written on a scroll of paper, for example. Speak this spell aloud:

Bygones be and lovers part,
I'm asking you to leave my heart.
Go in peace, harm to none.
My new life is now begun.

Go outside and, using your sacred bolline, cut off the string and toss it away along with the memento where it will no longer inhabit your living space. You should feel freer and lighter immediately and will attract many new potential paramours now that you are not weighed down by lost love.

Cleansing Winds Heart-healing Rite

Helping a jilted friend get over a bad relationship is good medicine, which can be therapeutic for you, as well. Recently, a brilliant male co-worker of mine was "dumped" unceremoniously by a woman he had been seeing for two years. As I witnessed him sink quickly into a deep depression, I felt compelled to help by using this heart-healing rite. I knew my friend walked to work each day, so, following the spell, I scattered the petals of one flower near his office front door so he would step on them and release their curative powers. I left the other rose on his desk. His spirits improved that very day. The healing of his heart had begun and each day, he had more spring in his step.

2 long-stemmed white roses

Take the petals from one rose, and bless them, chanting:

Eastern wind, wild and free,
Help _____ [friend's name] to see,
A better love will come from thee.

Scatter the petals somewhere that your friend goes often, for example outside their house or place of work. Give the other rose to your friend.

New Moon Charm for Banishing Heartbreak

Any new moon is the perfect time to create a new opportunity. Clear away relationship "baggage" with this banishing spell. If you have been hurt emotionally, this will clear it, fast.

A clear glass bowl filled with 2 cups (480ml) of water

A silver spoon

A salt shaker

Palo santo incense

2 white candles and 2 black candles

Place the clear glass bowl of water on your altar. Set a silver spoon beside the glass bowl along with a salt shaker. Light the cleansing palo santo incense, the two white candles, and the two black candles. Pour salt on the spoon, sprinkle the salt into the water and stir with the spoon clockwise. Recite aloud:

Hurt and pain are banished this night;
Fill this heart and home with light.
With harm to none and blessings to all.
So mote it be.

After a few moments of contemplating the candle flames, recite the spell again. Using the silver spoon as a snuffer, extinguish the candles. Toss the bowl of water out on the street in front of your house, near a drainage grate. All your love troubles should drain away by the end of this lunar cycle.

Getting Grounded in Yourself: Chakra Centering Visualization

The best way to prepare for personal ritual is to center yourself. I call this "doing a readjustment," and I believe this is especially important in our overscheduled and busy world. Doing a readjustment helps pull you back into yourself and gets your priorities on track again. Only when you are truly centered can you do the genuine inner work of self-development that is at the core of ritual.

Centering takes many forms. Experiment on your own to find out what works best for you. My priestess pal Kat, for example, does a quick meditation that she calls "the chakra check-in." The chakra system comprises energy points in the astral body, an energetic aura attached to your physical body that is associated with various endocrine glands in the physical body. My friend closes her eyes and sits lotus-fashion (with her legs crossed, feet on thighs—but if you are on a bus or about to attend a meeting, you can do this centering exercise just sitting down, feet on the floor—and visualizes the light and color of each chakra. She brings to mind each chakra and mentally runs energy up and down her spine, from bottom to top, pausing at each chakra point. After she does this a few times, a soothing calm surrounds her. I have seen her perform her "chakra check-in" at trade shows and in hotel lobbies, surrounded by the hubbub of many people. She is an ocean of calm at the center of a storm. By working with your chakras, you can become much more in touch with your body and soul.

* The **root chakra** is at the base of your spine and is associated with passion, survival and security, and the color red.

* Above it is the **sacral chakra** in the abdominal region, which corresponds to physical urges, such as hunger and sex, and the color orange.

* The **solar plexus chakra** is associated with personal power, and the color yellow.

* The **heart chakra** is the emotional center, for all strong feelings from love and happiness to the opposite. It is also associated with spiritual development, the higher self, and the color green.

* The **throat chakra** is considered the center of communication, and is blue in color.

* The **third eye chakra** is located in the center of your forehead and is associated with intuition, and the color indigo.

* The **crown chakra** at the very top of your head is your connection to the universe, and is violet in color.

Prior to performing a ritual, try this centering exercise. Take a comfortable sitting position and find your pulse. Keep your fingers on your pulse until you feel the steady rhythm of your own heart. Now begin slowly breathing, in rhythm with your heartbeat. Inhale for four beats, hold for four beats, and then exhale for five beats. Repeat this pattern for six cycles. People have reported that although it seems hard to match up with the heartbeat at first, with a little bit of practice, your breath and heartbeat will synchronize. Your entire body will relax as you are filled with calm.

Crown Chakra Tonic for Insight

This magical hair tonic will clear your mind, awaken your senses, and open your crown chakra, preparing the way for telepathic insight.

2-ounce (55ml) squeeze bottle

4 drops rosewood essential oil

2 tablespoons rosemary essential oil

A palmful of plain unscented hair conditioner

Timing: Ideally, perform this ritual when the sun or moon is in the truth-seeking signs of Gemini or Sagittarius for greatest effect.

Combine the oils and conditioner in the bottle. Shake well and pour onto your freshly shampooed hair while singing:

Sweetness, born of Rose,
Fly me on the wings of dreams.
We are made of sacred earth, purest water,
Sacred fire, wildest wind.
Blessing upon me. Blessing upon thee.
So mote it be.

At the very least, you will have visions and great clarity. You might even realize your true destiny. Wear your new wisdom gloriously, like a crown.

Guardians Circle Incantation

This little spell will take you far inside yourself. It will greatly empower you and instill in you a much deeper understanding of who you are and what you are here to do. Each of us is as individual as a snowflake, and our souls are imprinted with a stamp of specialness. The closer you get to the revelation of your soul's mission, the more you will know why you are here, and more importantly, what you are here to do. While the preparation takes a bit of time, the incantation is 5 minutes of pure magic.

Compass

1 votive candle

Pine essential oil

A 1 quart (1 liter) glass jar

Incense

Timing: The best time to perform this spell is during the new moon, when the night sky is at its darkest.

Go outside and find a solitary space in which you can cast a circle. Use the compass to find true north. When you feel comfortable and safe to begin, cast a circle of energy in the center of the circle. Anoint your candle with the essence of pine, a tree that stays strong, green, and alive all through the winter. Place the candle in the glass jar and light it, setting both carefully and securely on the ground. Then light the incense with the flame of the candle and stick it into the ground beside the votive candle. Breathe slowly and deeply; make yourself mindful that you are here in the darkest night, celebrating the sacred. As you breathe, look at the majesty of nature and the world around you. Feel the ground beneath your feet. Listen to the silence that encompasses you. Now open your heart completely to the awesome power of the universe and the magic both inside and outside of you. Touch your third eye, the chakric place in the center of your forehead. With your eyes closed, speak aloud this rhyme:

Here beneath the moonless sky,
I open my heart and wonder why
I am here.
Tonight, I will learn
The reason why I yearn
To serve the Goddess and the God.
This night, I'll hear the reason
I serve this darkest winter season.
Guardians, I call on you now!

Remain at the center of the circle and keep your eyes closed. You may hear an inner voice, or you may hear an outer voice right beside your ear. Listen calmly, staying centered with your two feet on the ground. You will know when it is time for you to seal the circle and leave with your new message and mission. When you move, you will initiate the closing of the circle. Thank the guardians as you close the sacred space, being sure to leave everything exactly as you found it. Incense, jar, compass, candles, and matches all leave with you.

When you return home, write your message on a slip of paper and place it on your altar, where it will be hidden from any eyes but yours. Place the candle, jar, and any remaining incense on your altar and burn it for a few minutes each dark moon night.

Final thought: You may also want to begin a special journal of your thoughts, inspirations, and actions regarding the message you received. You have now embarked on an exciting new phase of your life's journey. Your journal will help you as you make discovery after discovery. Your journal may evolve into a Book of Shadows, or it may one day become a book like this!

Rite for Welcoming Spirits

We can all use more benevolent energy in our lives. Some angels may take human form, such as a friend who is always there in a crisis. Others are hovering above in the ether and can be invoked with a few words and a focused intention. Use this spell when you need a guiding hand and angelic assistance.

1 white and 1 blue candle (these are angelic hues)

Rosemary essential oil

Frankincense and myrrh incense

Celestite, a sky-blue crystal associated with angel energy (amethyst can substitute)

Anoint both candles with the rosemary essential oil. Light the white candle and use it to light the incense. If you were unable to acquire any frankincense or myrrh incense, you can use rosemary incense or light a rosemary branch in a fireproof glass or clay dish. Now light the blue candle with the white one and place them on either side of the crystal. Breathe deeply and speak this spell aloud to invoke the celestial guardians.

Guardians, I call upon you now
To bring aid and angelic blessings
By earth and sky, I invite you now
To point me to all that is good
And protect me from all that is not.
With gratitude to the heavenly host.
So mote it be.

Witch Craft: Angel Accessing Charm for Protection

In your travels along the sacred path, you doubtless have gathered up many natural treasures, such as seashells, driftwood, crystals, and small pebbles. You can create a simple "Angel Accessing Tool" from your collection of nature's blessings. Make an amulet any time you want to gather up the good energy of those unseen who can help and protect you (and drive away the not so helpful energy). Here's how to make an amulet you can hang whenever you need to call upon angelic aid.

Sections of string, at least 6 inches (15cm) in length, one for each crystal

Small chunks of crystal (celestite, amethyst, aquamarine, muscovite, morganite, and selenite can all help you make contact with your guardian angels)

A stick (a small piece of sea-smoothed driftwood is perfect)

Tie a piece of string around each chunk of crystal. Attach each string to your stick of wood so the crystals are hanging from the stick. Hang your amulet anywhere in your home you want to "make contact."

Once you have crafted your magical tool, you should store it in a safe place and bring it out when you really need angelic intervention. When I lived in a big city that had lots of car break-ins, I made one for my car and the era of broken windows ended for me. I recommend one for your office space, too. We all need work angels! You can welcome unseen and benevolent spirits into your home and life with this conjuring charm.

Soothsayer Stone: Choosing and Using a Crystal Ball

When selecting a crystal ball, your choice should not be taken lightly. This is a very personal tool that will become instilled with your energy. Crystal balls have their own authority and they can strongly influence the development of our psychic abilities.

You should think of the crystal as a container that houses your energy, so make sure it feels right for you. The crystal should feel comfortable to hold—not too heavy and not too light. You should not allow anyone else to touch your crystal ball. If someone does touch it, place the ball in a bowl of sea salt overnight to cleanse it of outside energy and influence. Quartz crystal balls have inherent power, so you have to practice working with them first. Pure quartz crystal balls can be quite expensive, but the price is worth it if you are serious about harnessing your intuition and using it for good. And don't expect your experiences to be like the movies! Most of the people I know who use crystal balls, including many healers and teachers, see cloudy and smoky images.

Work with a partner to sharpen your psychic skills. Sit directly across from your partner with the crystal ball between you. Close your eyes halfway and look at the ball and into the ball while harnessing your entire mind. Empty out all other thoughts and focus as hard as you can. You will sense your third eye, the traditional seat of psychic awareness, begin to open and project into the crystal ball. By practicing this way, you will train your mind. The patterns you see will become clearer and your impressions more definite. You should trust that what you are seeing is real and find a place of knowing. For me, my gut seems to be an additional center of intuition. I just "know in my gut" when something is amiss. Verbalize to your partner what you see, and then listen to your partner as they reveal their visions to you.

You should also do crystal ball meditations on your own. In a darkened room, sit and hold your crystal ball in the palms of both hands. Touch it to your heart and then gently touch it to the center of your forehead, where your third eye is located. Then hold the ball in front of your physical eyes and, sitting very still, gaze into it for at least 3 minutes. Envision pure white light in the ball and hold on to that image. Practice the white-light visualization for up to a half hour and then rest your mind, your eyes, and your crystal ball. If you do this every day, within a month you should start to become adept at crystal-ball gazing.

When we gaze into a crystal ball, it is possible to see into the fabric of time, both the past and the future. At first you may be able to see a flickering, wispy, suggestive image. Some of you may be able to see clearly defined visions on your first try. Most of us have to practice and hone our attunement to the energy of the ball. You must establish clearly your interpretation of what you see. Many psychics use a crystal ball in their readings, and some report seeing images of clients' auras in the ball. Projecting information about people's lives is a huge responsibility, so you need to feel sure about what you are reading. Learn to trust your body's center of intuition.

Darning Your Aura: Crystal Combing

We have all encountered psychic vampires, who tear away little pieces of your chi, or life force, leaving holes in your aura (etheric body). You can identify the places that need patching because they will become noticeably cold as you pass a crystal over them.

Pick your favorite stone from amethyst, citrine, or any quartz and run it all around you at a distance of about 3 inches (7.5cm). Make note of the cold spots and lay the crystal on those places for about 5 minutes, until the spot feels warmer. This repairs the holes in your aura and you should begin to feel a pleasant sense of renewed wholeness once again.

Another wonderfully soothing technique is crystal combing. Take a piece of pink kunzite and brush it in gentle, slow, downward strokes from the top of your head, the crown chakra, to the bottom of your feet. The next time you feel overwhelmed by anxiety, try this and you will feel more relaxed and in control afterward.

Kunzite is also a heart mender, which works with the heart chakra to bring inner peace, clear away old romantic wounds, and get rid of emotional baggage. While lying down you can place a chunk of kunzite upon your chest, meditate with it, and feel the healing energy flow in.

Your Psychic Shield

You would not leave your house on a cold windy day without a sweater or jacket, right? I highly recommend you do not leave your house on a Monday morning without a psychic shield—you'll thank yourself later. If every work week feels like a challenge with a huge workload, tons of meetings, presentations, calls, and interactions, you should erect a protective shield so you can do good work but emerge unscathed from all busyness and business with others.

Visualize whatever feels like a secret defense against unwarranted psychic intruders. Some folk see big castle doors or a drawbridge, others utilize an enclosing egg, and I have even heard of a big silver blanket as a shield, but I prefer a kind of "force field" shield that I put up or take down. I also use a mental hooded robe that I wear anytime I go out in a group where I feel unsure about the people. In my mind, I cloak myself in my silver robe and do a brief silent meditation. Also, the best defense is a strong, positive attitude and sense of self. The more you practice your meditation and creative visualization, the greater your skill will grow.

Mondays Are Made for Magic

Monday comes from "moon day" and is ruled by the moon goddess known variously as Diana, Cybele, Artemis, and Selene. This first day of the work week is associated with all the hues of blue, from sapphire to pearly iridescent. This is the day for intuition, deep reflection, and love, especially loving your own true nature.

The Sacred Seven

This simple spell acknowledges the life force and the cycles of nature that give rise to our creativity.

On a Monday, light seven purple candles to represent the days of the week, and say aloud:

We begin by honoring the sun;
We begin by honoring the light.
We light these candles for our friends,
Our families, those we love.
May the light of these candles draw the power
of nature into our hearts;
May the light of the candles inspire us to help and never harm;
May each of the seven days be radiant with the
Light from every start.
Blessed be.

Extinguish the candles and keep them for another Monday ceremony.

CHAPTER 6

PROMPT PROSPERITY

The Secrets of Luck and Abundance

For centuries, witches have known that luck is neither random nor mysterious. Thanks to the wise women in my family who shared their "trade secrets" openly, I learned very early in life that I could manifest my will through the tools of magic. When in a pinch, I have used witchcraft to replenish the coffers. I have also used prosperity spells to find a good home, attract job opportunities, and help others. As soon as you approach your prosperity consciously, you will see that you have the power to choose abundance. And when you increase your material prosperity, you reduce the need to worry about just getting by day to day, and you can move on to achieving true prosperity: expanding your mind through learning, pursuing your pleasures, spending time with family and friends, and enjoying your life.

Pointing the Way to Prosperity

For prosperity spells, I recommend having a wand made from ash (*Fraxinus excelsior*). Ash grows fast and its seedlings root everywhere, so it's persistent. Use ash for prosperity and self-improvement.

If your prosperity wand can fit well on your altar, I suggest keeping it there and you can also use a crystal at the end, such as citrine (see page 166) to boost the power of any ritual you are working on your altar. For example, whatever ritual elements symbolize money, point your wand with its crystal at those for an extra charge.

Money Flow: Feng Shui Fountain

Water fountains are good feng shui and can enhance your prosperity quotient. For those of us who can't pull off a fountain in our home or garden, this works just as well to get the money flowing.

At least 8 small, smooth river rocks
A large green bowl or tall vase
Enough water to fill the container
Your prosperity wand (see above)

Stand in the front door area of your home and identify which is the far-left corner. This is the prosperity area and, therefore, the perfect place for this ritual. Place the smooth river rocks in the bottom of the bowl or vase and carefully pour in the water so you avoid spilling any. Take up your wand and speak aloud:

In the name of the Goddess, I dedicate this space.
Peace and prosperity flows throughout this place.
Everyone here will enjoy abundance and grace.
With harm to none. So mote it be.

Gently stir the surface of the water with your wand so it swirls and circles. Repeat the spell, then bow and say thank you to the energies of abundance.

Remove the stones from the vessel and pour the water onto the roots of the nearest tree or one of your larger potted plants, ideally right outside your home. Keep the stones in the far left corner of your home for continual good feng shui. This will keep the flow of abundance in your personal space.

Prosperity Pouches: DIY Charm Bags

A charm bag is a little bag or pouch filled with objects charged with magic for a specific intent. You can charge the objects with magic by placing them on your altar for 24 hours or, for a 5-minute fix, use spellwork, as suggested here.

12 inches (30cm) green cord or string

1 green candle

Thyme or cinnamon incense

A small muslin or cloth bag/pouch (that could fit in the palm of your hand)

Bolline

1 cinnamon stick

1 teaspoon dried basil leaves

3 pebble-size crystals of green jade, peridot, or turquoise

Set the cord or string aside and place all the other items on your altar. Stand at your altar and light the candle and incense. Pick up the pouch and smudge it in the sweet smoke of the incense while saying the following spell:

My life is blessed and this I know.
Into this bag, prosperity will flow.
I see the future is bright wherever I go,
My life is blessed; this much I know.
With harm to none; so mote it be.

Using your bolline, cut the cinnamon stick into 3 pieces. Cut the green cord or string into 3 pieces. Place the basil, crystals, and cinnamon into the pouch. Now take the pieces of green cord and, one at a time, tie the end of the bag securely. Keep it with you in your pocket and into your life, money will flow.

151

Prosperity Intention

I had a very scary financial situation in 2008, right before the "credit crunch," which became known as The Great Recession. I had moved in with my fiancé and we bought a home together at the very edge of San Francisco with a teeny Pacific Ocean view. He worked in tech and his earnings were much more than mine but we never gave it a second thought. It was a modest home but we loved it and I threw myself into gardening, sowing herb beds, arranging sacred shrines and all the lovely aspects of Wiccan nesting.

He passed away unexpectedly before our marriage and before the shock of that even subsided, I was hit with bills for funeral arrangements, house payments, hospital bills, and myriad unforeseen expenses that left me close to broke and going underwater on the mortgage. I was deep in grief but knew I had to get myself out. I needed to sell the house as quickly as possible, find an affordable place to rent in the San Francisco Bay Area, pack up and move and also earn more money.

In times like these, group magic is called for. I asked a group of girlfriends who had been very supportive during all the travails if they would meet with me once a week for Intending. They were happy to help and curious, too. The first time we met, we all set an intention for a desired outcome or need—I couldn't help but notice that all their intentions were more achievable than mine—and brought potluck food to share.

We began our group ritual by going round the circle and stating our gratitude for all we do have in our lives. Next we each set our intention regarding our desired need or outcome. Kara said, "I need a free bookcase for my baby's books and toys. I ask this for the good of all. And so it is."

Our circle was a small and loving group of five women so it took less than 5 minutes for us to set our individual intentions. Afterward, I spoke my deep thanks for their support and we shared the food.

The next morning, I got a call from Kara. She said, "You are not going to believe this but I walked outside of our apartment building and there was a bookcase. It looks new and it's white and exactly what I had in mind. Wow, that intending stuff really works!" Kara is exactly right. The group magic of setting intentions that are good for you and also for everyone on the planet really does work. It took a month but I got everything on my list, too. Goddess is good. Friends are great.

Set Your Intention to Be a Master Manifestor

I learned the art of intention-setting some years ago and quickly incorporated it into my morning rituals. Upon waking, sometimes even before I open my eyes, I set my intention for the day—it only takes a minute! It can be about work, financial challenges, a problem I am dealing with, relationships, health, hopes and dreams—anything, as long as it is also for the good of all. It has become a morning prayer for me, quick and quiet. I simply state my intention, such as, "I intend that my presentation today at work will go really well and I will feel joy as it is happening and set the stage for success for this product launch, for the good of all. I am grateful for this wonderful day. And so it is." During the peak of my money woes, I would get very specific and set intentions for the exact amount of money I needed to make the mortgage payments, pay credit card bills, etc. Granular detail is good when manifesting so it is fine to say how much you want when intending with money.

Keep these other tips in mind:

* Avoid using words with any negative charge to them, such as "can't," "but," and "won't," and amplify your intention with a statement of gratitude immediately after.

* Always state your intention as if it is happening now and not in the future. Be specific and intend without limit.

* Your intentions do not always have to be personal to you and intending for the greater good of all contributes to a positive global shift.

* By setting intentions every day, you will soon become a master manifestor. I intend that for you!

Money-attraction Herbs

As a kitchen witch and gardening enthusiast, I am always seeking to learn more about how the power of herbs, plants, roots, and flowers can be used in the craft. Grow your wealth, literally, with these handy herbs.

* **Allspice berries** bring good luck: Gather seven berries and place in a small pouch to carry in your pocket or purse for a week. On the seventh day, place the berries in your fireproof dish and burn them with cinnamon incense while making your wish for whatever you want.

* **Basil** is a major herb of abundance as well as love. Drop a few fresh basil leaves on the floor of your kitchen and sweep them out of your home with your magical broom while speaking this charm: "Scarcity is out the door; no longer will I be poor. Health and wealth, be here now. Harm to none, so mote it be."

* **Cinnamon** has come to be called the "Sweet Money Spice" and this delightfully scented herb is a bringer of luck and will make a business more prosperous. Sprinkle a dash of ground cinnamon on the threshold of your front door, store, or business and watch the wealth walk in!

* **Cloves** are herbs of good fortune and even help in gambling. They also bring people together and bind them. If you need to turn your luck around, use cloves in spellwork as an herbal element or in incense or potpourri to create energy of abundance.

* **Ginger root** can speed up any magic. You can grind up the dried ginger root into powder; adding this to your money-attraction spells will bring the funds much sooner. Ginger tea brings money your way, briskly!

* **Nutmeg** is another spice beloved by gamesmen and gamblers. Carry a whole nutmeg in your pocket and your luck will improve the same day.

* **Thyme** is a common herb that will attract money to your home. Every time you cook with it, you draw abundance and wealth toward you. Drink thyme tea for a quick fortune turnaround and fast money magic with this spell, "It is time for money to come my way; good luck is mine. Money thyme is mine with blessings for all."

Coin Conjuration

We all have unexpected expenses that come out of the blue—car repairs, medical bills, or helping a loved one in need. I had the latter with my family and had to reach deep into my coffers to heed the call. When you need to recover quickly financially, this coin spell will fill the bill, literally.

Athame

3 gold (or yellow) candles

Frankincense or myrrh incense

3 yellow or gold-colored crystals, such as tiger's eye, amber, citrine, yellow jade, or another favorite of yours

3 pieces of yellow- or gold-colored fruit, such as yellow apples or oranges

13 coins of different denominations

A green or gold jar with a lid

Timing: Perform this spell on the evening of a new moon or during a waxing moon phase.

Make a quickie temporary altar wherever you pay your bills and handle your money—maybe it is your desk or perhaps the kitchen table. Use your athame to create the circle of magic in this soon-to-be-sacred space. Place the candles, incense, crystals, and fruit on the temporary altar and arrange them into three groups so each group contains a crystal, piece of fruit, and candle. Light your candles and the incense. One by one, take the coins in your hand and pass them through the incense smoke. Place the coins in the jar. Now take the crystals in your hand and pass them through the smoke, then place in the jar and seal. Pick up one piece of fruit at a time and touch to your third eye (in the middle of your forehead). Pray aloud:

This offering I make as my blessing to all,
Comfort and earthly gifts upon us shall fall.
Fill my coffers with silver and gold.
In this time of great need, I will be bold.
For the good of all, young and old.
Fill my coffers with silver and gold.
And so it is.

Extinguish the candles and incense and place on your altar for future use, as well as the vessel containing the coins. When you go to sleep, dream of everyone you love, including yourself, receiving a harvest of material and spiritual wealth.

Lucky Seven Almond Attraction Spell

In your pantry, you have much that you need to attract whatever you want more of into your life—love, money, a new home, a new job, increased creativity. The jar of almonds on your shelf is filled with sheer potential, and not just for delicious snacks or dessert. If you are fortunate enough to have an almond tree, harvest your own, but store-bought almonds are just as good. The great psychic Edgar Cayce ate five almonds a day for cancer prevention and believed this healthy nut contained great power. Almond oil is excellent for your skin, applied lightly as a self-blessing. A dab of almond-attraction oil will go far for you, too, in this easy and effective spell.

If you are feeling a financial pinch, try rubbing a dab of almond oil on your wallet and visualize it filling up with money. To engender greater and long-lasting change, perform this spell.

Take seven green votive candles, seven almonds, and seven flat, green leaves from a plant in your garden—ivy or geranium are excellent choices. On your kitchen table, arrange the candles in a circle, placing them on the leaves. Anoint each candle with a dab of almond oil, which works swiftly as it is ruled by Mercury, the god of speed, swift change, and fast communication who operates in the element of Air. Place the almonds in the center. At 7 a.m. or 7 p.m. for seven days, light a candle and eat one almond. Then incant aloud the words on the left.

Luck be quick, luck be kind.
And by lucky seven, good fortune
will be mine.
As above, so below,
The wisdom of the gods shall freely flow.
To perfect possibility, in gratitude I go.

Each day, as the clock strikes seven, perform your ritual. Later, you can count your blessings; there will be at least seven!

Basil and Mint Money Bags

Rather than chasing money or possessions, you can simple draw them toward you with wisdom from days gone by. Fill a tiny green pouch with the herbs basil and mint, three cinnamon sticks, one silver dollar (or a shiny pound coin), and a green stone—peridot or a smooth, mossy-colored pebble of jade would be perfect. The untrained eye might perceive this as a bag of weeds and rocks but any kitchen witch recognizes this is a powerful tool for creating dynamic change in your life and attracting good fortune.

Prepare your attraction pouch during a waxing moon; the strongest power would be when the sun or moon are in Taurus, Cancer, or Capricorn. Hold the pouch over frankincense incense and, as the smoke blesses the bag, you speak:

The moon is a silver coin; this I know.
I carry lunar magic with me everywhere I go.
Blessings upon thee and me as my
abundance grows.

Carry this power pouch with you as you go about your day—to work, to the store, on your daily walks, to social events. Soon, blessings will shower down upon you. You might even receive a gift or literally find money in your path.

Magical Thinking: The Manifestor's Mindset

I first heard the wisdom of the visionary teacher and writer Louise Hay 25 years ago when my dear friend Duncan gifted me his well-worn cassette tape of her speaking about how to develop a mindset of abundance.

Duncan patiently explained to me his takeaways from Hay's wisdom. For example, when paying bills, instead of resenting the company that supplies your water and electricity, write the check, seal the envelope and say aloud, "Thank you [whomever your check is for], for supplying me with power for my home and trusting me to pay you. Blessings to you!" We began a ritual of walking together to the mailbox and pronouncing our gratitude to all the recipients of our money, adding the finishing touch of kissing the stamped envelopes and saying "Thank you!" before dropping them in.

Soon, it began to work for me, as I had a far better attitude about paying my bills. I realized that paying on time saved late fees and was finally able to budget and handle my money in a smarter way. Most surprising of all, I stopped being filled with dread and worry when bills came in and started paying them the same day they arrived, whenever possible.

That was in the early 1990s, when we walked to the mailbox for our 5-minute gratitude ritual. Nowadays with all the instantaneous ways of sending money and electronic payments, it might be closer to a 5-second ritual. However, you can still get into your manifestor's mindset and express thanks before you hit "send." The attitude of abundance that stems from this mindset is like a muscle; the more you use it, the stronger it will be and the more manifestation you will see.

Louise Hay is no longer with us but her brilliance and generosity of spirit remain and, thanks to all her books and audios, we can learn from her still.

Celebration of Plenty: Morning Meditation

True abundance comes from looking at what you have, rather than focusing on what you lack. This spell will begin each day with magic.

Upon waking, take time to reflect on the good things in your life. After meditating upon those blessings, say this spell aloud:

Today and every day,
I see the richness of life.
I thank you, Goddess,
For all the gifts and beauty in my world.
Today, I will share my blessings with others
and honor you.
I see plenty for all. Blessed be.

Luck by the Cup

When you are crafting money magic, it is good to get into the manifesting mindset with some prosperity tea.

1 tablespoon dried rose hips

1 tablespoon dried chamomile

1 teaspoon orange peel

2 cups (480ml) freshly boiled water

A teapot

A green mug

Strainer

1 cinnamon stick

Steep the rose hips, chamomile, and orange peel in the freshly boiled water in the teapot for 4 minutes. Pour the tea into the mug through the strainer, and stir widdershins, or counterclockwise, with the cinnamon stick for a moment. As you drink, visualize the abundance coming into your life.

May Magic: Flower Moon Invocation

The fullest phase of the moon can be the time for the greatest of magic—you can conjure your heart's desire and tackle the "big things" of life, whether that be a problem to resolve, a major life transition, such as seeking a new job or home, whatever your truest wish. This gorgeous spring Flower Moon provides an optimal opportunity to strive for the new, to initiate a phase of transformation in your life that will last long after the full moon has waxed into darkness. This invocation honors the season of spring, planting seeds of positive change in your life that will bloom for years to come. Start by gathering red and green apples, candles of the same colors, a few grains of seed corn from a gardening store or natural grocery, along with three stalks of lavender and a long strand night-blooming jasmine. Leave these offerings on your altar all day.

Through the power of Earth and Air, Water and Fire.
As I bite this fruit of knowledge,
I am thus inspired.
All possibilities are before me. And so it is.

When the full moon of May reaches the highest point in the night sky, light one red and one green candle on your kitchen altar. Wind the jasmine and lavender into a crown for the top of your head, breathing in the lovely scent the flowers produce. For three minutes, visualize your desired change for this spell. Holding an apple in each hand, speak the words of the spell on the left while circling the candlelit altar clockwise three times.

Eat from both apples until you are fully satisfied, then bury the corn seeds and the cores near your kitchen door or the rightmost corner of your garden. With the spring rains, your intentions will come into being. By the fall full moon, you will be harvesting the bounty of change from this spell, with great gratitude.

Basil Pesto Perfection

This recipe is simply scrumptious and a bargain to boot. You can gather a nice big bunch of basil leaves from your kitchen garden or greengrocer. It is the perfect dish to serve when you need to brew up some good money-mojo. Based on basil's other benefits, it's also great after an emotionally hard week, as it is a bringer of peace.

Rinse the leaves in cold water and place them on a clean dish towel to air dry. Place the pine nuts and the garlic on a baking sheet in the oven at 375°F/190°C/gas mark 5 for 5–10 minutes or until the pine nuts begin to turn slightly golden. Do not wait until they turn brown, though.

Place the pine nuts and garlic in a blender or food processor with the Parmesan. Before you put the lid in place, cut the lemon in half and squeeze out a nice dollop of fresh juice and grind in a healthy dash of sea salt. Blend away until you have a lovely green pesto sauce you can put on anything. Perfect pesto in 10 minutes flat!

Boil up a pot of pasta while you are concocting the blissful basil and you will have a sumptuous weeknight supper for the family on the table so quickly, they will be sure you are using witchcraft.

2 cups (100g) packed fresh basil leaves

½ cup (70g) pine nuts

3 garlic cloves, peeled

½ cup (50g) Parmesan cheese, grated

Juice of ½ fresh lemon

Sea salt

Serves 6

Finding Lost Treasure: Potion of Plenty

The humble dandelion, considered a bothersome weed by some, hides its might well. Dandelion root tea can help you find lost treasure, money, wallets, even people. When you drink it in direct moonlight, sleep will be sweet and clues and messages will appear in your dreams.

Mortar and pestle

2 tablespoons dried dandelion root

2 cups (480ml) freshly boiled water

A teapot

Oven mitts

A large Pyrex bowl (or other heatproof bowl)

A strainer

With your mortar and pestle, grind the dandelion root and steep in the freshly boiled water in your teapot. Pour into the bowl through the strainer. Now slip on your oven mitts and hold the bowl in your hands. Say aloud seven times what you are looking for. Afterward, pour the potion onto your front stoop or the steps in front of your home. What you are looking for will return to you.

Money Magic Bath

You can almost seal the deal before a job interview with this prosperity ritual. This spell is most effective if practiced on a new or full moon Thursday night, but can certainly be used whenever you need.

Pour 6 drops of mint, verbena, or apple essential oil into running bath water. You can also use all three. Turn off all lights, step into the tub, and bathe by the light of a single green candle. As you close your eyes, meditate on your true desires. What does personal prosperity mean to you? What do you really need and what do you really want?

When you are clear about your answers, focus on the candle flame while whispering:

Here and now, my intention is set.
New luck will be mine and all needs will be met,
With harm to none and plenty for all.
Blessed be. So mote it be.

Cash in a Flash:
Crystal Currency

Another charm for solvency is to take seven tiny
turquoise stones in the palm of your hand and
speak this wish-spell aloud:

Luck be quick,
luck be kind,
and, by lucky seven,
good luck will be mine.
Blessed be.

Place the seven small stones in your wallet or purse;
more cash is on the way.

The Giving-tree Spell

In Celtic lore, certain kinds of trees were called wishing trees. Taoists refer to them as money trees; either way, they can be "giving" trees (see below).

A plain white piece of paper
A pen
1 stick of jasmine or rose incense

Write your wishes for prosperity and luck on the paper. Specificity is key and you should include the details of what you are asking for. If you need more money to buy a new laptop, write that down. It can be more than one wish. Now, fold your wish paper into a square as small as possible and bury the paper in soil at the bottom of a giving tree. Choose from the list of magical trees below, or trust your intuition in arboreal matters.

Light the incense stick, place it by the buried paper and pray aloud:

Tree of plenty; I ask you to give
More abundance and money so I can live,
I ask for _____ [fill in blank] as it will truly help me.
With harm to none, so mote it be.

Repeat the spell twice and your wish will be put into effect.

GIVING TREES

Willow for healing broken hearts

Apple for divination and spellwork

Cherry for romance

Oak for strength and lust

Peach for love magic

Olive for peace

Aspen for sensitivity

Eucalyptus for purification

The Wealth of Wildflowers

Pagans revere poppies for their money magic. If you have a yard or any strip of ground you can garden, even a nearby meadow, buy poppy seeds and simply scatter half of them in early spring. Save the other half for the spell below. Soon, you will have a wealth of wildflowers. No doubt, you will be rewarded with the beauty and abundance of poppies for many years to come.

Poppy seeds
A small plain paper envelope
A pen

Place the remaining poppy seeds in the envelope. Bless the envelope by chanting aloud:

Poppy, gold like the sun,
Thank you for the new fortune I've won.
With these words, this spell is sealed. And so it is.

Now, write the charm you have spoken on the envelope. Seal the envelope and place it in your wallet, behind your paper money. Your fortunes will begin to change as soon as the envelope is sealed.

Directing Your Destiny

By now, you may know exactly what kind of wood you want for your wand (see page 22). Now, you can select the ideal crystal to power your tool of magic. Below is a guide to the magical powers inherent in different crystals so you can choose which ones to use in your spells and rituals. Abundance rites will be enhanced with bloodstone or citrine while calcite and chalcedony offer protection. See which stones work best for you.

Supernatural Stones

* Amethyst for balance and intuition
* Aventurine for creative visualization
* Bloodstone for abundance
* Calcite for warding off ill fortune
* Chalcedony for power over dark spirits
* Citrine for motivation and success
* Fluorite for contacting fairies
* Garnet for protection from negativity
* Hematite for strength and courage
* Jade brings powerful dreams
* Moss agate for powers of persuasion
* Quartz crystal for divining your dreams
* Rhodochrosite for seeing life's true purpose
* Watermelon tourmaline for seeing the future

Lucky Wishing Charms

Many of us don't realize that the classic charm bracelet is decorated with magical symbols representing the wearer's wishes.

* For prosperity, such as before a job interview, when asking for a raise, or if you find yourself in arrears, wear a coin.
* For love, try a heart.
* For creativity on a project, choose a pen or artist's palette.

Silver Ring of Power Spell

A pure silver ring worn on the right pinky finger can bring both physical and psychic power. To enhance the magical power, have the ring engraved with your birth sign or astrological glyph and the sacred pentagram.

To instill the ring with protective power, clasp it over your heart and call out:

Ring of power, shield and encircle me. Blessed be.

Terrific Talismans: Personal Totems for Success

If you are preparing a major presentation to the team at work, showing your paintings to a curator, practicing for your dance performance, or pitching your book idea to a publisher, you can wear a talisman of your own making to ensure a positive outcome. Many performers, athletes, and musicians have lucky pieces of clothing or some token that gives them the courage to put themselves forth in the best possible manner. I have a Big Sur jade pendant on a length of leather that I wear on auspicious occasions such as these. Jade is about abundance and it is so smooth to the touch that it doubles as a soothing worry stone for me. I highly recommend you carry a jade talisman as it can be a major magical tool that can bring good fortune to you for many years.

To maximize the power of your jade talisman, consider the following tried-and-tested suggestions. Keep in mind that this will work even better if you place the item on your altar to imbue it with the right energy.

* For a speech, presentation, performance, or show, wear a red garment.

* If you are preparing for a potentially lucrative deal, you must wear green.

* If you are trying to empower someone to see and share your creative vision, blue is the right hue for you.

Super Sunday Affirmations

Sunday is the day of our greatest star, Sol, otherwise known as the sun, with colors of gold, orange, and radiant white. This is the time to rest and renew, indulge in creativity, and enjoy the fruits of this life. Sundays are an ideal time for boosting your confidence and esteeming yourself.

On a Sunday morning after your ablutions, when you are your most well-rested, freshly scrubbed, shiniest self, speak these powerful words:

I am amazing and awesome
I grow in wisdom each day.
I am succeeding.
I am prospering.
Blessings to all and blessed be me.

Feel free to create your own affirmations, if you are so inspired. This Sunday ritual feels simply divine and truly is empowering. If it works as well for you as I suspect it will, you may want to incorporate it into every Sunday morning. Blessed be!

Sanctified Sunday: Sure Success Incantation

Here is one of the ways I got a great job on my first day in San Francisco, despite the fact that I wasn't really qualified and looked like an absolute hayseed after driving cross-country for four straight days from Appalachia. I was broke and fresh out of grad school with no real experience but I created some luck for myself. You can, too, with this surefire spell.

Light a gold candle on a Sunday night before you undertake your job hunt or whenever you are about to go on a job interview. Repeat this incantation three times while holding a vision of your desired job:

I see the perfect job for me; I see a place of plenty.
Upon my heart's desire, I am set;
My new boss will never regret.
This job will come to me NOW.
Harm to none I VOW.
So mote it be.

CHAPTER 7

THE WHEEL OF THE YEAR

Lunar Power and Special Days

The human heart longs for ritual and ways to mark life passages.
The pagan calendar handles that wonderfully by reminding us of the
cycles of nature, the phases of the moon, and the importance of
spending time in community. Nearly all our modern high holidays have
ancient roots in farming customs and fertility rituals to ensure good
crops and plenty for all. Lunar festivals, solstice seasonal galas, and
major sabbat celebrations, as well as personal rites of passage, all call
for ceremonial magic, family feasts, and acknowledgment of the
natural world. This is the time to count our blessings and share them.
Observing these high holy days with the circle rites, magical foods, and
pagan prayers herein assures that your home will be a temple
dedicated to joy for many years to come.

Your Moon Phase Guide

The proper phase of the moon is essential for spellcraft. Each lunar cycle begins with a "new" phase when the moon lies between the sun and the earth so the illuminated side cannot be seen from earth. The moon gradually "waxes" until it has moved to the opposite side of the earth, and its lit side faces us in the "full" moon phase. It then begins to "wane" until it reaches the new moon phase again. The entire cycle takes around a month, during which the moon orbits the earth.

Performing a spell at the optimal time in the lunar cycle will maximize your power. As you read the spells in this book, keep this essential approach to magic in mind.

Matching Your Spells to Moon Phases

* The new moon is an auspicious time for a fresh start.

* The crescent moon, which appears seven days before and after the new moon, is the time for productivity and creating positive energy.

* While waxing, the moon grows steadily larger and is good for spellwork toward completing goals and building toward an outcome.

* The full moon is a great teacher with a special message for each month.

* The waning moon is the time to wind down any personal challenges and see them to an end.

New Moon, New Friends

When I moved to San Francisco, I didn't know a soul, but I used this tried-and-tested trick to fill my life with friends.

1 candle of any color or size
Your favorite incense

Timing: Try this on a new moon Friday (Freya's Day, which is ruled by Venus, is ideal for fun, love, flirtation, gossip, and good times).

Light the candle and incense. Breath in the sacred smoke and dance around, arms held upward, joyously. Say aloud:

I call upon you, friend Freya, to fill my life with love and joy.
I call upon you, Goddess,to bring unto me that which I enjoy
In the form of people, wise and kind.
This I ask and give thanks for, blessed be.

This resulted in me having friends who have stuck with me through thick and thin; I can count on them for boundless love and they bring so much joy to my life.

Inspired Clarity: Breath of the Gods Incense

Burn this mixture of incense on your altar to generate a positive and peaceful atmosphere to set the stage for your ritual. Rose hips and mint are for heart, enthusiasm, and keen thinking. The yellow candle, yellow rose, and the yellow citrine crystal are used to symbolize intelligence and mental clarity.

1 tablespoon dried rose hips

1 teaspoon fresh or dried mint

A charcoal cake for burning incense

A fireproof clay or glass dish

A yellow candle

Neroli essential oil

A yellow rose bud

1 cup (240ml) of fresh water in a bowl

A citrine crystal

Using your mortar and pestle, grind together the rose hips and the mint. Once they are nicely mixed, place the herbs on a piece of charcoal in a fireproof clay or glass dish. Light a yellow candle anointed with neroli oil and place a single yellow rose in a vase to one side of the incense burner. On the other side, place the bowl of water with the citrine crystal in it. Light the incense and breathe in. The word "inspire" comes from the Greek word for "breath of the gods," so allow this divine essence to fill you with grace.

Timing: Perform this rite during the new moon, when the moon is dark and not visible.

Crescent Moon Magic

This is the perfect time to lay plans for all good things you desire in this phase of increasing.

A pure white garment

A moonstone of any size

A short piece of string

Timing: The ideal phase for this spell is when the crescent moon is waxing.

In the first quarter of the moon, don your white shirt or dress, and carry the moonstone along with you in your pocket or on a pendant. Take a late afternoon walk in a park or a meadow among wild weeds, flowers, and grasses, and gather a few as you stroll to make a bouquet. Choose a resting place and sit where you can see the crescent moon. Take your flowers and grasses and bind them with the string. Hold your newly made bouquet in your right hand. Hold your moonstone in your left hand and concentrate on your desired outcome—creative fulfillment, greater happiness, or perhaps the release of anger. Chant aloud:

Luna, in your seventh heaven, I invoke you now.
Brighter than any star, you are.
I will sing your magic song, if you but show me how.
I will walk your sacred path, if you but show me where.
Be here now.

Arms outspread, eyes on the moon, repeat the chant three times. As the moon shines brighter, so will your spirit.

Magical Cookery

The kitchen is the heart center of every home. No matter how beautifully we decorate parlors, living rooms, and dens, people gravitate right back to the kitchen. Why is that? Kitchens are where the magic happens! Food is made here and, along with it, plenty of love is dished up in heaping servings. With kitchen witchery, recipes and preparations go into spellwork, concocting cures right out of the cupboard, preserving and canning food grown in the garden, drying herbs for teas and cookery, and unleashing the power of the pantry. In creating enchanted edibles, we can use the best and freshest ingredients for healthy, hearty dishes, but we can also add in some very special ingredients with our magical intention in accordance with the celestial calendar and by utilizing the ingredients with the desired properties.

I had the great good fortune to grow up in the countryside on a farm. Much of what I know I learned from my witchy aunt—about which herbs to gather in the wild, which foods to cook for love, money, luck, health, and in celebration of the high holidays. It is exciting to go to the garden, the grocery store, or the farmer's market and bring home the ingredients for positive life change. In addition to the secrets to magical cooking, I learned from this wise woman that the first task to undertake is to clean your kitchen and purify it. If anything needs repairing, fix it. Any utensils, pots, or pans that are dented can be donated. If your kitchen curtains look shabby to your eye, make or buy new ones. If there is a bag of rice or beans past its prime, compost away. You should clean the cooking space in both the practical sense and also cleanse it in the magical sense. Prepare your kitchen to be used for the purpose of magic.

Harvest Moon Herb Soup

After the September equinox signals the change of seasons from summer to fall, you should start making pots of this seasonal meal, which is a guaranteed crowd pleaser. This autumnal soup is just as pleasing to the cook as it can be a quick supper, leftovers for lunch, and easily frozen for meals on the go. It is simple and delicious. On the eve of the first full moon of fall, gather the ingredients and prepare. Refrigerate overnight and the flavors will "marry" together to intensify and become an even more savory supper to serve to loved ones on this harvest moon night.

In a large iron skillet or frying pan (preferably well-seasoned by use in your kitchen) fry the leeks in the olive oil until they become soft and translucent. Add in the chopped garlic and cook until it is also soft and wafting a wonderful scent into your kitchen. (Recipe continues overleaf.)

3 large leeks, thinly sliced

¼ cup (60ml) virgin olive oil

2 fresh garlic cloves, chopped

8 cups (2 liters) water

1 butternut squash, peeled, seeded, and coarsely grated

1 carrot, thinly sliced

4 large floury potatoes, such as Idaho or Maris Piper, or sweet potatoes, peeled and cut into small, spoon-sized chunks

¼ cup (5g) fresh sage, finely chopped

¼ cup (10g) fresh chives, finely chopped

Salt and pepper

¼ teaspoon celery salt

Serves 8

Transfer to a soup pot, oil and all, and add the water, heating to a boil. Add all the veggies and herbs and turn the heat down to a simmer for 45 minutes. Test the potatoes to see if they are soft enough—do this by mashing with a wooden spoon. If they are still a bit hard, simmer for another 5 minutes. Turn the heat down very low, then season with salt and pepper. Add the celery salt as the last element of the year's abundance.

Serve in clay, wooden, or ceramic bowls by the light of a brown or yellow candle. A chunk of homemade bread would be the ideal seasonal accompaniment.

Moon Drop Savory Scones

1 cup (125g) all-purpose (plain) flour

¼ teaspoon baking soda (bicarbonate of soda)

1 teaspoon baking powder

¼ teaspoon salt

3 tablespoons (40g) cold unsalted butter

⅔ cup (160ml) buttermilk

Makes 10 biscuits

Serve these piping hot and straight out of the oven; this is a batch of ten delicious biscuits (scones). Better still, they're drop biscuits, which means there's no need to roll and cut the dough. If you are having more than five folks over for supper, double up the ingredients. These Moon Drop biscuits are excellent for dipping into soup and stews.

Preheat the oven to 450°F/230°C/gas mark 8. In a medium bowl, combine the flour, baking soda, baking powder, and salt. Whisk gently to blend the ingredients. With two knives, cut the butter in until the mixture looks like coarse meal. Add in the buttermilk and stir until it is blended, but do not over stir. Drop heaping tablespoons of the mixture onto an oiled baking sheet; you should separate the biscuits by 2 inches (5cm). Bake for 12 minutes and pull the biscuits out once they are a light-golden, buttery brown.

"A kitchen witch preparing a ritual meal for her circle is engaging in one of the oldest forms of enchantment by harnessing the energies in each ingredient and cooking with sacred intention."

Lunar Lore

Many of our full-moon names come from medieval books of hours and also from the Native American tradition. Here is a list of rare names from the two traditions, which you may want to use in your lunar rituals.

* **January:** Old Moon, Chaste Moon; this fierce Wolf Moon is the time to recognize your strength of spirit

* **February:** Hunger Moon; the cool Snow Moon is for personal vision and intention-setting

* **March:** Crust Moon, Sugar Moon; the gentle Sap Moon heralds the end of winter and nature's rebirth

* **April:** Sprouting Grass Moon, Egg Moon, Fish Moon; spring's sweet Pink Moon celebrates health and full life force

* **May:** Milk Moon, Corn Planting Moon, Dyad Moon; the Flower Moon provides inspiration with the bloom of beauty

* **June:** Hor Moon, Rose Moon; the Strawberry Moon heralds the Summer Solstice and sustaining power of the sun

* **July:** Buck Moon, Hay Moon; this Thunder Moon showers us with rain and cleansing storms

* **August:** Barley Moon, Wyrt Moon, Sturgeon Moon; summer gifts us with the Red Moon, the time for passion and lust for life

* **September:** Green Corn Moon, Wine Moon; fall's Harvest Moon is the time to be grateful and reap what we have sown

* **October:** Dying Grass Moon, Travel Moon, Blood Moon, Moon of Changing Seasons; the Hunter's Moon is when we plan and store for winter ahead

* **November:** Frost Moon, Snow Moon; Beaver Moon is the time to call upon our true wild nature

* **December:** Cold Moon, Oak Moon; this is the lightest night of the shortest day and is the time to gather the tribe around the fire and share stories of the good life together

Holiday Rituals

Sabbats are the holy days for each season of the year, in accordance with the celestial spheres above. Some of these holy days celebrate the arrival of spring and the start of new growth, while others mark the harvest in preparation for the dark and chilly days of winter. Nearly all our festivals have roots in the ancient rites based in fertility and the hopes of abundant farm crops.

Humankind first marked time by the movement of the stars, Sun, and Moon in the sky, which also informed the designation of constellations and astrological calendars. Candlemas, Beltane, Lammas Day, and All Hallow's Eve are the major sabbats. The lesser sabbats, listed below, are the astrological markers of new seasons:

* Ostara: March 21, also known as the Vernal or Spring Equinox

* Litha: June 21, commonly known as the Summer Solstice

* Mabon: September 21, best known as the Autumnal Equinox

* Yule: December 21, is the Winter Solstice

Candlemas: The Coming Season

Candlemas, on February 2, also known as Imbolc, is the highest point between the winter solstice and spring equinox. This festival anticipates the coming of spring with banquets and blessings. Tradition holds that milk must be served and modern pagans have expanded that to butter cookies, ice cream, and cheeses; and any other related food should be shared. It is an important time to welcome new members of your spiritual circle and new witches into a coven. Candlemas is a heartwarming occasion, but it is still a wintry time so kindling for the hearth or bonfire should include cedar, pine, juniper, and holly along with wreaths of the same to mark the four cardinal points, alongside white candles in glass votives. Strong incense such as cedar, nag champa, or frankincense will bless the space. The circle leader shall begin the ritual by lighting incense from the fire and, facing each direction, and saying:

Welcome Guardians of the East, bringing your fresh winds and breath of life. Come to the circle of Imbolc.
Welcome Guardians of the South, you bring us heart and health. Come to the circle on this holy day.
Welcome Guardians of the West, place of setting sun and mighty mountains. Come to us.
Welcome Guardians of the North, land of life-giving rains and snow. Come to our circle on this sacred day.

The leader should welcome each member of the circle and speak of the gifts they bring to the community. Everyone should acknowledge one another with toasts and blessings and break bread together in this time of the coming season.

181

Cakes and Ale: Saturn-day Night Fever

Here is a pagan party plan, which is wonderful for weekend evenings. You can add many embellishments, such as important astrological or lunar happenings, but you should gather your friends or coven and celebrate life any Saturday night of your choosing. If the weather is warm enough, have the festivities outside. Otherwise, make sure to choose an indoor space with enough room for dancing, drumming, and major merriment. Ask each of your guests to bring cake, cookies, and candies of their choice along with their favorite beer, wine, mead, cider, or ale, and sitting cushions. Place the offerings on a center-table altar and light candles of all colors. Once everyone is seated and settled, the host or designated circle leader chants:

Gods of Nature, bless these cakes.
That we may never suffer hunger.
Goddess of the harvest,
Bless this ale,
That we may never suffer thirst. Blessed be.

The eldest and the youngest should serve the food and drink to all in the circle. Lastly, they serve each other and the leader chants the blessing again. Let the feasting begin!

Spiritual Spring Cleaning: the Bean Blessing

The change of season at the Vernal Equinox, on March 21, brings about the need for new energies, which you can engender with cleansing. Here is an ancient way to cast out "the old" and bring in glad tidings and positive new beginnings for your friends and family.

Grab a bag of beans from your kitchen and invite your circle over. In ancient times, many pagan peoples, from Incans to Egyptians and Greeks, believed beans contained evil spirits, so this rite comes from that lineage. Go to your roof or the highest point of your house which you can get to safely and give everyone a handful of beans. Each person throws one bean at a time, calling out whatever they need to bid goodbye to— a bad habit, nightmare job, whatever your personal demons may be. After everyone has tossed the negativity and discord away, celebrate the clean slate. Fun note, if you toss lentils into a barren field in the spring, by fall, you will be able to harvest enough for many pots of soup!

✳

SPROUT INTO SPRING
ALL YEAR-ROUND

Sprouts are immensely nutritious and fairly effortless to grow: add one teaspoon of seeds to a quart jar filled with water and cover with cheesecloth. After 24 hours, turn the jar upside down and drain. After at least 2 hours, refill and repeat this process twice a day for 3–5 days. You'll have a rich repast for salads, sandwiches, soups, and stir fries. Try these seeds for endless healthy options: sunflower, mung bean, broccoli, quinoa, lentil, radish, mustard, alfalfa, red clover, and fenugreek.

Your Personal New Year: Birthday Rite

The anniversary of your birth is like a new year, when everyone can start again, wearing new clothes, beginning life anew with a fresh attitude and bright hopes. Invite your friends and loved ones over for this special day.

Plenty of candles

1 cup (240ml) of water

A dish of salt

Incense

A new piece of clothing (such as a scarf) or a new item of jewelry

A plate of cakes and sweets to share

Light as many candles as you can in the room where you are performing this ritual. Create a circle of candles, and create a sacred space by having a symbol of each element in your circle: a dish of salt for Earth, a cup of water, incense for Air, and a candle for Fire. Sit lotus-style in the center of your circle and relax in the flickering candlelight. Feel the presence of the four elements and the balance they create. Notice how warm and alive the room feels. Notice how the gentle, flickering candlelight makes all feel safe. As you bask in the atmosphere of the loving candlelight, say to each of your guests, one by one:

I am grateful to have you in my life. May the power of Earth, Air, Fire, and Water bless you.

When you have finished your statements of appreciation, purify the new piece of clothing or item of jewelry by passing it through the smoke of the incense. Then put on your new piece of jewelry or clothing, saying:

With this act, I declare this new year is here, and see the future bright with hope.

Stay within your circle of light for 5 minutes. Then share the food and libations and relax with your special friends. Leave some of the cake or sweets as an offering to the gods in thanks for your new life in the coming solar year.

A Home for the New Soul: Baby Blessing

If any ritual is meant to be swift, it is the blessing of a new baby into the family and tribe. The baby will often quite vocally let everyone know when time is up and even that just adds to the fun!

A bright blue cloth for swaddling

A vial of water that has been blessed

You don't need any other supplies, just loving, happy people with the new parents and their child. A priestess or elder conducts the ceremony and begins by welcoming all and speaking a personal intention for the new parents and the baby. She then carefully swaddles the baby in the blue cloth and begins singing this song:

We all come from the Goddess
And to her we shall return.
Like a drop of water,
Flowing to the ocean.

As below, so above.
Mother, father, daughter, son,
Wisdom's gift shall be your own.
Crone and sage, youth and sage
We welcome you with all our hearts of love.

Gently pour a drop of the blessed water on the baby's head and chant the blessing again.

At this point, the little one will doubtless be ready for a nap and the tribe should go for a joyful feast.

Beltane Eve

Beltane, celebrated on April 30, is without doubt the sexiest of pagan high holidays, and it is anticipated greatly throughout the year. Witchy ones celebrate this holy night, and it is traditional for celebrations to last all through the night. This is a festival for feasting, singing, laughter, and lovemaking. On May Day, when the sun returns in the morning, revelers gather to erect a merrily beribboned Maypole to dance around, followed by picnics and sensual siestas. The recipe below is befitting this special time of the year when love flows as freely as wine.

Beltane Brew

1 quart (1 liter) honey

3 quarts (3 liters) distilled water

Herbs to flavor, such as cinnamon, nutmeg, vanilla, according to your preference

1 packet (7g) of active dry yeast

Honeyed mead is revered as the drink of choice for this sexiest of pagan holy days. It is an aphrodisiac and signals the ripeness of this day devoted to love and lust. This recipe is adapted from a medieval method.

Mix the honey and water. Boil for 5 minutes. You can add the herbs to your liking but I prefer a tablespoon each of clove, nutmeg, cinnamon, and allspice. Add a packet of yeast and mix. Put everything in a large container. Cover with plastic wrap and allow to rise and expand. Store the mix in a dark place and allow it to set for seven days, ideally at the beginning of a new-moon phase. Refrigerate for three days while the sediment settles at the bottom. Strain and store in a colored glass bottle, preferably green. You can drink it now but after seven months, it will have gained a full-bodied flavor. Always keep the mead in a cool dark place.

Nonalcoholic Mead

Boil all the mixed ingredients for five minutes and let cool. Bottle immediately in a colored glass jar. Keep this in the fridge to avoid fermentation and enjoy during any festive occasion. This is a healthy and refreshing way to celebrate.

1 quart (1 liter) honey
3 quarts (3 liters) distilled water
½ cup (120ml) lemon juice
1 lemon, sliced
½ teaspoon nutmeg
pinch of salt

Hoof and Horn Rite

Ideally, you would celebrate outdoors, but if indoor-bound on Beltane Eve, pick a place with a fireplace and have a roaring blaze, so celebrants can wear comfy clothing and dance barefoot. Ask them to bring spring flowers and musical instruments, plenty of drums! Place pillows on the floor and serve an ambrosial spread of finger foods, honeyed mead, beer, spiced cider, wine, and fruity teas. As you light circle incense, set out green, red, and white candles, one for each participant. When it is time to call the circle, raise your arm and point to each direction, saying "To the east, to the north," etc., then sing:

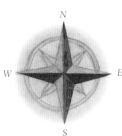

Hoof and horn, hoof and horn, tonight our
spirits are reborn [repeat thrice]
Welcome, joy, to this home. Fill these friends
with love and laughter. So mote it be.

Have each guest light a candle and speak to the subject of love with a toast of Beltane Brew. Drumming and dancing is the next part of the circle. This is truly an invocation of lust for life and will be a night to remember for all. Now rejoice!

The Crown of Cronehood: A Ritual of Honoring

Women should feel good about aging. They should celebrate long, full lives, and be respected and honored for the wisdom they bring to the community. Croning rituals, such as this one, are the signal to the group that a woman has ascended into a new role of service and leadership to the family, the tribe, the village, and the sisterhood. Elders say this coming of age occurs at the woman's second Saturn return, which is at age 58 to 60, but modern women now often decide for themselves.

While this ritual can last as long as is needed, the actual crowning lasts for only 5 very magical minutes.

A flowering branch

A crown or tiara (you can easily obtain one at any costume shop), placed on the altar table

Enough candles to represent every year of the crone's life

Upon the arrival of the soon-to-be-crowned crone, the eldest woman present should take a flowering branch, dip it in water, and sprinkle it on the crone's head, just a few drops, and speak this blessing:

I bless you in the name of the Goddess.
I bless you in the name of Mother Earth.
I bless you in the name of every woman.
Sister, do you accept the role of teacher and leader as crone?

The crone responds. If she accepts the title, then the eldest woman says:

She is crowned.

The eldest woman places the Crown of Cronehood upon the new crone's head. Now everyone should speak together:

We gather together to celebrate that [new crone's name] is entering the Wise Age.

Now the eldest woman and the youngest woman present light the candles. After everyone has spoken her tribute to the crone, she can speak her thanks. When the newly crowned crone has spoken from her heart, she ends with "Blessed be to all." Food is then served, and it should be a birthday party to remember for a lifetime.

Sacred Grove Solstice Spell

Celebrating the season of the sun, on June 21, is best done outdoors in the glory of nature's full bloom. If you have a forest nearby or a favorite grove of trees, plan to picnic and share this rite of passage with your spiritual circle. Covens often have a favorite spot. All the better if a great oak is growing there, the tree most sacred to druids. Gather the tribe and bring brightly colored ribbons and indelible markers. Form the circle by holding hands, then point to east, south, north, and west, chanting:

> *We hold the wisdom of the sun,*
> *We see the beauty of our earth.*
> *To the universe that gives us life, we return the gift.*
> *Deepest peace to all,*
> *And we are all one. Blessed be.*

Each member of the circle should speak their wish for the world, themselves, or loved ones and write it on a ribbon. One by one, tie your ribbon to a tree. Each flutter of the wind will spread your well wishes.

Summer Solstice Pudding

Inspired by a traditional recipe from Kent, known as "The Garden of England," this summer pudding brings forth the taste of the season, simply sublime.

Combine all the fruit and sugar in a saucepan and gently boil for 3 minutes. Squeeze in the juice of half a lemon. Line a big bowl with the bread, overlapping to form a crust. Pour in the fruit mix. Add one last bread slice to cover the mixture and place a saucer on top with a weight on it to press down. Cover with plastic wrap and chill in the refrigerator overnight. Before serving, turn the dish upside down and the pudding will slip out in a half-circle shape. Top with fresh whipped cream and a few berries and mint leaves as garnish. This cool treat could not be easier. Each spoonful is filled with the sweetness of summer.

1 pound (450g) fresh mixed berries—strawberries, raspberries, blueberries, blackberries

1 cup (225g) diced fresh peaches, plums, nectarines

¼ cup (50g) sugar

juice of ½ lemon

10 slices crust-less bread (or 15 biscuits or shortbreads)

Lammas Day: Harvesting Happiness

This major sabbat, on August 2, denotes the high point of the year; the crops are in their fullness, the weather is warm, and the countryside is bursting forth with the beauty of life. Pagans know we have the heavens above to thank for this and the gods of nature must be acknowledged for their generosity with a gathering of the tribe and a feast, ideally in the great outdoors.

Ask invitees to bring harvest-themed offerings for the altar: gourds, pumpkins, bundles of wheat stalks and corn, fresh pickings from their garden, and food to share in thanksgiving made from the same—pies, tomato salads, cucumber pickles, green beans, corn pudding, watermelon, lemon cakes, apple cider, and beer brewed from wheat, hops, and barley. This celebration of the harvests of the summer season should reflect what you have grown with your own hands. Fill your cauldron or a big, beautiful colored glass bowl half-full with freshly drawn water and get packets of tiny votive candles to float in it. At the feast table, make sure to have a place setting for the godly guest Lugh, who watched over the plantings to ensure this bounty. Place loaves of Lammas bread by his plate.

When all guests have arrived, everyone should add a food offering to the plate of the god and light a candle to float in the cauldron. Cut a slice of Lammas bread for Lugh and begin the ceremony with this prayer of thanks:

Oh, ancient Lugh of the fields and farms,
We invite you here with open arms,
In this place between worlds, in flowering fields of hay.
You have brought the blessings we receive this Lammas Day.

Begin the feast and, before the dessert course, everyone should go around the table and speak of their gratitude for the gifts of the year. Storytelling, singing, spiral dances, and all manner of merriment are part of Lammas Day.

Lugh Lore: Guardian of the Harvest

The "Shining One" from the Celtic mythology, Lugh is the warrior sun god and also guardian of crops. The Lughnassa is a festival in honor of the harvest god, taking place at the beginning of every August. Lammas, which means "loaf mass," was the Anglo Saxon's fete for the first harvest of the year and included sport competitions in addition to feasting, dancing, and ritual. The Scottish caber toss, a log-throwing contest, derives from this sort of yearly folk Olympics. These two early-August festivals were conflated over the centuries, with Lammas becoming ingrained in the pagan calendar.

At the end of summer and fall, kitchen witches should hold rituals of gratitude for the abundance of the crops and for the gift that is life. This will keep the flow of prosperity coming to you and yours. Lugh also has domain over late-summer storms, so anyone experiencing drought or wildfires can pray to Lugh for rains to come.

Lammas Day Bread

This recipe makes 1 large or 2 regular loaves.

Mix the dry ingredients in a large bowl. Add the peanut butter and honey to the hot milk and stir to combine. Cool the milk mixture to warm and pour into the dry ingredients. Knead for 15 minutes, adding the extra flour, if needed, to make a smooth and elastic dough. Oil the surface of the dough, cover with plastic wrap or a damp kitchen towel, and let rise in a warm place until it has doubled in size; this usually takes 90 minutes. Punch it down and shape into your desired loaf size. Allow to rise again, covered in a warm place.

Bake in a preheated oven at 375ºF/190ºC/gas mark 5 for 30 minutes until golden brown and hollow-sounding when you rap on the bottom.

2 cups (270g) whole-wheat flour, plus an additional ½ cup (70g) set aside

2 cups (270g) bread flour

¼ cup (35g) toasted sesame seeds

2 tablespoons active dry yeast

2½ teaspoons salt

2 tablespoons peanut butter

2 tablespoons honey

2 cups (480ml) milk, scalded

Fall Equinox Festival: Mabon

Your kitchen is not just where you prepare meals, concoct healing tonics, and craft enchantments; it is also a temple with an altar where you honor spirit. This change-of-seasons sabbat of Mabon, on September 21, marks the turning of weather and the other face of nature. Mark the four directions on your altar with a loaf of bread in the east, a bowl of apples in the south, a bottle of wine in west, and an ear of Indian corn in the north.

✳

LEAFY LEGEND: GRABBING LUCK BY THE HAND

Here is a sweet bit of alchemy available to all, handed down from medieval times. Wise women of yore taught their children to look for falling leaves. To catch one in your hand is the best kind of luck, directly from Mother Nature herself. Carry it with you for a season and you will be safe from harm and find gifts in your path. If you are especially blessed to catch two leaves in one season, the second is for your companion of destiny. You will be bound by both feeling and fortune.

Corn Moon Clan Pot

This can be a nice meal to serve during the Corn Moon and ritual feasts involving growth and transformation. Corn is associated with self-sustainability and fecundity, both of people and of the land. Sharing this dish on the September full Moon is a time to remember and be grateful for all we have sown and all we have reaped to acknowledge the continuing cycles of life. Kids will love this "a-maize-ing" dish—they will ask for seconds!

In a large pan over high heat, combine the pasta, tomatoes, enchilada sauce, and water. Heat to a boil, then reduce the temperature to medium heat; add the chicken, black beans, corn, and salsa. If your family likes it extra hot, throw in some green peppers to turn the heat up a notch. Reduce the heat to low, cover, and let simmer for 20 minutes, or until the pasta is tender and cooked through. Top with the cheese and the herbs; place the lid on the pan. Let the cheese melt in for 5 minutes and serve up this global crowd pleaser in heaping bowls.

2 cups (200g) dry penne pasta

8 ounces (225g) diced tomatoes

1 jar enchilada sauce, 8 ounces (225g)

1½ cups (350ml) water

2 cups (250g) shredded, cooked chicken

1 can black beans

1 cup (175g) fresh (or frozen) corn

2 tablespoons salsa

2 tablespoons hot sauce

½ cup (50g) Cheddar cheese, grated

Basil, cilantro (coriander), chives, avocado, and sour cream

Samhain: All Hallows' Eve

Halloween, on October 31, stems from the grand tradition of the Celtic New Year. What started as a folk festival celebrated by small groups in rural areas has come to be the second largest holiday nowadays in North America and is increasingly gaining popularity in the UK and the rest of Europe. There are multitudinous reasons, including modern marketing, but I think it satisfies a basic human need to let your "wild side" out, to be free and more connected with the ancient ways. This is the time when the veil between worlds is thinnest and you can commune with the other side, with elders, and the spirit world. It is important to honor the ancestors during this major sabbat and acknowledge what transpired in the passing year as well as set intentions for the coming one.

This is the ideal time to invite your circle; the ideal number for your "coven" is 13. Gather powdered incense, salt, a loaf of bread, goblets for wine, and three candles to represent the triple goddess for altar offerings. Ideally on an outdoor stone altar, pour the powdered incense into a pentagram star shape. Let go of old sorrows, angers, and anything not befitting new beginnings in this new year. Bring only your best to this auspicious occasion.

Light the candles and say:

In honor of the Triple
Goddess on this sacred night
of Samhain,
All the ancient ones,
From time before time,
To those behind the veil.

✳

A DIFFERENT KIND OF CANDLE MAGIC

Drips, drops, and spills of candle wax come with the territory of witchery. Scraping doesn't work and leaves a bigger mess. Here's the trick: take a damp terrycloth towel and place over the wax spill; put a hot iron on it for a minute and the wax will be pulled up into the cloth. Abracadabra: the wax has vanished.

Rap the altar three times and light the incense. Say this blessing aloud:

For this bread, wine, and salt,
We ask the blessings of Mother,
Maiden, and Crone,
And the gods who guard the
Gate of the World.

Sprinkle salt over the bread, eat the bread, and drink the wine.

Each of the celebrants should come to the altar repeating the bread and wine blessing. After this, be seated and everyone in turn should name those on the other side and offer thanks to ancestors and deities. This can and should take a long time as we owe much to loved ones on the other side.

New Year's Kitchen

A form of magic handed down from antiquity is to have a domestic goddess figure in your home; archaeologists have found them amongst the most ancient artifacts. It is a good energy generator to have such a figurine decorating your kitchen altar. The most important consideration is to choose the divinity with which you feel the deepest connection.

Global Goddesses Every Witch Should Know

* **Chicomecoatl:** this Aztec corn goddess brings prosperity to farmers

* **Dugnai:** this Slavic deity is a house guardian and blesser of breads

* **Fornax:** here is the goddess of all ovens, Roman in origin; she guards against hunger

* **Frigg:** this benevolent Nordic being watches over the domestic arts (including love)

* **Fuchi:** the Japanese invoke her when they need fires—cooking fire, campfire, and celebrations

* **Hebe:** daughter of Hera and Zeus, this goddess of youth is also a cupbearer who can bless your chalices and kitchen ritual vessels

* **Hehsui-no-kami:** in Japan, she is the kitchen goddess and she can be yours, too

* **Huixtocihuatl:** the Aztec goddess of salt is one to turn to and thank each and every day

* **Ida:** the subcontinent of India looks to her who rules fire and spiritual devotion

* **Ivenopae:** the Indonesian mother of rice helps at harvest time, feeding millions

* **Li:** nourishing fires is the charge of this Chinese goddess

* **Nikkai:** the first fruits of the season are the gifts of this Canaanite holiness

* **Ogetsu-hime:** this dependable deity is the Japanese goddess of food

* **Okitsu-hime:** revered from ancient times is this Japanese kitchen goddess

* **Pirua:** Peru's mother of maize is sacred to all who rely on her for survival

* **Pomona:** the fruit goddess of Roman times has domain over gardens and orchards

* **Saule:** this Baltic benefic is a sun goddess who lights the hearth fires and all homely arts

Salt Dough Deity Recipe

A marvelous group ritual to hold is a "kitchen warming." Invite over a group of friends and bake up a batch of goddesses from the list on page 197 or your own inspiration. Salt dough is used to create lovely domestic sculptures, such as braided breads that are lacquered to decorate your domicile. This easy and fun approach will bless your homes for the seasons to come. You can double or triple the amounts based on how many goddesses are working together.

Mix the three ingredients together and then knead gently by hand, adding in teaspoons of additional water until the dough is completely smooth. Rest on a clean, dry wooden chopping board for half an hour. If you want to have colored dough, add in an organic food coloring, which you drop into the water at the beginning. Blue, green, yellow, red, orange, and purple are perfect to represent goddesses.

Shape your goddess as you see fit or use an image from a book that speaks to you. Once your goddess is sculpted, place her in the oven at a low temperature of 250°F/120°C/gas mark ½ and bake for at least 2 hours until the surface is firm to the touch. Take her out and let her cool, then decorate with paint, glitter, beads, jewels, and all the ornamentation suitable to her royal station.

I love the apple tree in my back yard. To honor the fruit goddess Pomona, I shape a simple image of her with an apple-wreath crown, painted red and green. When spring rains bring apple blossoms, I return Pomona to the tree over which she watches. Each year, there are more apples thanks to her generosity.

2 cups (270g) flour
1 cup (200g) salt
½ cup (120ml) water

✳

NUTTY BUT GENIUS

Before you have your circle over for festivities, you need to prepare the temple, your home. The humble walnut was sacred to King Solomon and grew in the Hanging Gardens of Babylon. Head to the pantry for this penny-wise preparation: you can remove marks from wooden furniture by halving a walnut and rubbing the edge along the grain of the wood. House magic!

Yule: Winter Solstice Bonfire

December is named for the Roman goddess Decima, one of the three fates. The word "yule" comes from the Old Norse *jol*, which means midwinter and is celebrated on the shortest day of the year, December 21. The old tradition was to have a vigil at a bonfire to make sure the sun did indeed rise again. This primeval custom evolved to become a storytelling evening and while it may well be too cold to sit outside in snow and sleet, congregating around a blazing hearthfire, dining, and talking deep into the night are still important for your community truly to know one another, impart wisdom, and speak of hopes and dreams. Greet the new sun with stronger connections and a shared vision for the coming solar year.

*

WINTER-IS-COMING ROOT ROAST

We live in a time when some of the very foods the early Yule celebrants feasted upon are having a renaissance—bone broths, root vegetables, and stone fruits. These are simple to prepare and share with the clan. The following root veggies are magnificent when roasted with rosemary for 40 minutes at 450°F/230°C/gas mark 8 with a drizzling of olive oil and salt: 2 pounds (1kg) mix-and-match medium-sized yams, potatoes, garlic, mushrooms, onions, parsnips, carrots, and beets. In the rare chance of leftovers, these can become the basis for a heart-warming soup or stew.

"The pagan path is not only about looking inward, but also about becoming attuned to the world around you—every leaf, stone, blade, flower, and seed; the highest calling of any Wiccan is to achieve harmony with the cycles of the natural world."

Journaling Your Spellcraft

The art and practice of modern Wicca is, at its core, an expression of your spirituality. While many of the sabbat celebrations and circle rites are gatherings of the tribe, much of your spellcraft will be performed by a coven of one—you. And it is the "inner work" of devising and creating personal rituals, tracking life cycles of the moon and stars, and recording your magical workings in your Book of Shadows that will encourage your deepest spiritual development. Your life is a work in progress and here is a record of it. The insights you gain from going back and considering all that has come before are priceless. Here should be your musings, invocations, hopes, and intentions. I call this the Journal of the Journey and it can take any form your imagination conjures, as long as the deep truths and revelations of your work are captured.

These next few pages of prompts are all for you to record your magical musings and inspired ideas. Keep these and look back now and again for reflection. You may discover that the entries penned in this journal were the first steps in renewal and new directions in your life. This record of your own wisdom is a priceless treasure.

Blessed be from my kitchen to yours!

*The new-Moon phase is the time for fresh ventures, renewing, cleansing, and clearing.
What seeds will you sow during this time for new beginnings?*

_____

_____

_____

_____

_____

_____

_____

_____

_____

_____

*A waxing moon is the time for abundance, attraction, and love magic. It can also heal rifts
and protect existing relationships. What do you want to attract during this time?*

_____

_____

_____

_____

_____

_____

_____

_____

_____

_____

_____

_____

_____

The full Moon shines a light on challenges in your life; now is the time to release and let go of anything causing problems. What are the issues or old patterns you should "catch and release"?

_____

_____

_____

_____

_____

_____

_____

_____

_____

_____

_____

The waning moon is a time to emphasize the positive by banishing the negative. Rid yourself of any unconstructive feelings, habits, health challenges, or thoughts; clear out the psychic clutter with the spells you have learned and replace it with good energy. What psychic clutter do you need to clear?

_____

_____

_____

_____

_____

_____

_____

_____

_____

_____

_____

Circles and group rituals often occur only on high holy days. What is some
of the solo spellwork you want to explore during the rest of the year?
What rituals would you like to design and create?

_____

_____

_____

_____

_____

_____

_____

_____

_____

Intention-setting is one of the most powerful ways through which you
can bring positive change into your life. It is a vital kind of inner-work.
What are your magical intentions and visions for the days and weeks to come?

_____

_____

_____

_____

_____

_____

_____

_____

_____

Conclusion: Fill Your Life with Enchantment

We are experiencing a witchy renaissance here in the early years of the twenty-first century. I get frequent requests from friends and, thanks to the quick connections of social media, questions via Facebook about how to handle the stress, strain, and busyness of modern life. I am honored to be able to help in any small way and am constantly seeking new methods for healing magic and insights and spells for sacred self-care.

One thing I do know, both from my personal experience and from my circle, is that spellwork and habitual ritual can be healing in and of itself. Rites and ritual gatherings regulate our lives, individually and as groups. Anthropologists, psychologists, and other students of the human race have shown that ritual has existed since the dawn of humanity and has always played an important role in culture. Scholars of the psyche, including Freud, who eloquently addressed the role of ritual, speak of the power of ritual and how it brings people together physically and emotionally. Ritual creates "communities" from which spring a sense of unity, harmony, and belonging.

These magical moments are very important; they signify that we have stepped out of the routine of the ordinary day to day and are exploring a higher consciousness. I believe a moment spent in ritual is embracing life itself. Even 5 minutes of sacred time can change your life for the better. And that is my hope for you: a life enriched through these easy enchantments and simple spells. May you enjoy much peace of mind, prosperity, love, and sheer joy!

Resources

Moon Phases and Lunar Astrology

Moon phases, Sun and Moon signs, and more: almanac.com/topics/astronomy/moon/moon-phase

The Old Farmer's Almanac is also available in print: store.almanac.com

Lunar lore, herbal lore, and astrological information: thewitchesalmanac.com

I also recommend *Llewellyn's Daily Planetary Guide* (published annually for the year ahead).

Crystals

Crystals, Tibetan rock salt, fossils, gems, and jewelry: crystalsbynature.com

Crystals, wands, crystalline statuary, and jewelry: crystalage.com

Petrified wood and fossils: www.fossilera.com/fossils-for-sale/petrified-wood

Birthstones, crystals, and lore: birthstonemagic.com

Essential Oils, Incense, and Herbs

Advice on using essential oils safely: www.aromaweb.com/articles/safety.asp

Essential oils, carrier oils, and soap- and candle-making supplies: junipertreesupplies.com

Incenses, burners, sages, and herbs: herbsandarts.com/incense-burners

Dried herbs, essential oils, floral waters, and books: scarletsage.com

A Witch's Calendar: Additional Sacred Days Celebrating Women

January 6—Feast of Goddess Sirona, the blessing of the waters

January 11—Carmentalia, a woman's festival celebrating women's mysteries, prophecy, and birth

February 2—St Brigid's Day when new witches are initiated with the waxing of winter light

February 14—Aphrodite's Week, a festival of love (now Valentine's Day)

March 30—Feast of Fertility, a rite of spring for planting and sowing

April 28—Festival of Flora, rituals of abundance for new flowers and vegetables

June 1—Festival of Epipi, an exhortation of the Full Moon and her mysteries

June 7—Vestalia, the festival of Vesta, the Roman goddess of home and hearth

July 7—Nonae Carpotinae, ancient Roman custom celebrating women, feasting under the fig tree

August 13—Festival for Diana, huntress and moon goddess, worshipped with fires and pilgrimages

August 21—Consualia, greeting the coming harvest with dances, feasting, song, and sport

December 19—Opalia observes Ops, the ancient goddess of farmers and fertility

index

Acknowledgments

Deep gratitude to publisher Cindy Richards and CICO Books for the great pleasure of working on this book, which is a thing of beauty and a visual delight. Belle Daughtry's photography and styling are brilliant and offer so much to readers. Emma Garner's luscious illustrations are simply delightful and, along with Emily Breen's and Eliana Holder's expert design, they bring the pages to life. I greatly appreciate how copy-editors Jennifer Jahn and Sophie Elletson spun my words into gold. I have much to be thankful for in my life and I count among my blessings the CICO "Dream Team." I have been writing and publishing for several years and I have never experienced such a plentitude of grace and good work. I am inspired by all of you!

Photography credits

All photography is by Belle Daughtry apart from the following:

pp. 129 and 142: Crystal photography by Roy Palmer
pp. 128, 168, and 184: Kate Whitaker